"Most of us are not called to [do great things, but to do small things] with great love. Written by a Little Sister of Jesus who follows the way of Charles de Foucauld, this book invites ordinary people to be alert to the contemplative dimension of everyday life. This is a spirituality of presence and friendship, of welcome and receptivity to the gift of God's love in 'the other'—especially those who are last, littlest and least in our midst."

— Michael Downey, author, *The Heart of Hope:*
Contemplating Life, Awakening Love

"Charles de Foucauld was one of the great spiritual masters of modern times. Through his witness countless people have rediscovered the face of Jesus in their neighbors and among the poor. In this invaluable guide to his life and message, Little Sister Cathy Wright has penetrated the heart of Foucauld's unique vision. More than ever, the world has need of his compassionate spirit."

— Robert Ellsberg, editor, *Charles de Foucauld: Writings*

"Cathy Wright, herself a Little Sister of Jesus, gives us a profile of and a spiritual meditation on Blessed Charles de Foucauld, who is, without a doubt, one of the premier spiritual masters of the modern era. Wright's book is crisply written, profoundly contemplative, yet extremely readable. Highly recommended."

— Lawrence S. Cunningham,
John A. O'Brien, Professor of Theology
The University of Notre Dame

CHARLES DE FOUCAULD

CHARLES DE FOUCAULD

Journey of the Spirit

By

Cathy Wright, lsj

Library of Congress Cataloging-in-Publication Data

Wright, Cathy, 1951–
  Charles de Foucauld : journey of the spirit / Cathy Wright.
    p. cm.
  Includes bibliographical references.
  ISBN 0-8198-1576-4 (pbk.)
  1. Foucauld, Charles de, 1858-1916. 2. Hermits—Algeria—Biography. 3. Foucauld, Charles de, 1858-1916—Meditations. I. Title.
  BX4705.F65W75 2005
  271'.79—dc22

                                    2005013265

Published by Pauline Books & Media, 50 Saint Pauls Avenue, Boston, MA 02130-3491.

Printed in the U.S.A.

www.pauline.org

Pauline Books & Media is the publishing house of the Daughters of St. Paul, an international congregation of women religious serving the Church with the communications media.

1 2 3 4 5 6 7 8 9   11 10 09 08 07 06 05

CONTENTS

Part One

—•—

UNDERSTANDING THE MIND AND HEART OF CHARLES DE FOUCAULD

Part Two

PRAYING WITH
CHARLES DE FOUCAULD

Preface

I FIRST MET CHARLES DE FOUCAULD about thirty years ago when I considered entering religious life and a friend told me to look into the Little Sisters of Jesus. I had never heard of Charles or of the Little Sisters. Both seemed exotic with their roots in the Sahara Desert, a world away from Washington, D.C., where I had grown up. For someone who had never gone further than a day's ride away from home, there I was, suddenly with the whole world broken wide open before my eyes and heart. I was hooked.

In the photos that the sisters showed me, I caught glimpses of relationships changing little corners of the world through "presence." I saw a way of life that was immersed in the everyday existence of people around the world, people from different races, faiths, and cultures, people who struggled with poverty and powerlessness. I saw pictures of the sisters' chapels: simple, prayerful spaces carved into the places where they lived, be it a tent, an apartment, a boat, or a trailer. I began to understand how contemplation of the Incarnation and the sacrament of the Presence of Jesus was a doorway into those relationships. It was also the mystery that rooted and supported the sisters' own search for the face of God.

Charles de Foucauld called this way of life Nazareth. He discovered it half a world away and a century ago. He struggled to give it a name at a time when there were no models to express what he was reaching for. As he grappled with questions of faith and with the world of his day, he lived with apparent failure and wrestled with doubt. Rather than cutting himself off from others in his search for God, the God whom he encountered in prayer led him to meet another people as brothers and sisters. Charles offered his life in the solidarity of that love.

This was no overnight transformation, but a gradual evolution in the life of a person, who tried to be faithful to grace. We see the evolution in every area of his life, from before his conversion until his death. As I look back on my own life, I understand this process better. We set out on a path, not knowing where it will really lead us, but trying to follow Jesus. We trust. The consequences of our choice to follow Jesus carry us beyond what we ever could have imagined on our own, into situations totally beyond us and into the depths of our own faith. One step leads to another, and we find ourselves in the midst of a mystery that, on the one hand, is so ordinary that we risk missing it and, on the other hand, when we take the time to ponder, is so overwhelming that we have few words to describe it.

Brother Charles fell in love with Jesus and spent his life seeking Jesus' face. He found it among the Muslim people of Algeria and allowed himself to be drawn beyond his preconceptions into a friendship with a people that can only be described as the Communion of Saints. In a world that is so divided and yet longs for the peace that such communion brings, I think that Charles has a word to speak to us today.

ACKNOWLEDGMENTS

IN WRITING THIS BOOK I HAVE DRAWN on many sources that are not available in the English language. Most of Charles de Foucauld's writings can be found in a series of books published by Nouvelle Cité, Paris, France. I am grateful to them for permission to quote from those sources, as well as to Les Editions du Seuil, Desclée de Brouwer, Les Editions du Cerf, Grasset, and the Archives for the Cause of the Canonization of Charles de Foucauld. Some translations exist in English, and I have included a bibliography of these at the end of this book. But for this book I have directly translated all texts from the original French.

I have also drawn on the collective wisdom of the communities founded on the spirituality of Charles de Foucauld. There are many unpublished writings and reflections that have remained internal documents and that form a basis for approaching his spirituality. A whole history of lived experience grows richer as we continue to draw new inspiration from Brother Charles' life for our mission today. I owe a great debt of gratitude to Antoine Chatelard, a Little Brother of Jesus, who over the years has done extensive research into the life and writings of Brother Charles. I have drawn on many of his ideas and extremely interesting work that has also not been published in English. Many thanks also to Little Sister Annie for her tireless work to share Charles' charism.

Thank you to the Daughters of St. Paul, who were the ones who approached me about publishing something about the spirituality of Charles de Foucauld on the occasion of his beatification. I would never have imagined or been able to do this on my own, and their encouragement and editorial expertise have been invaluable.

Thanks also are due to Msgr. Maurice Bouvier, Postulator of the Cause for Charles de Foucauld's Canonization and Administrator of the Archives, as well as to the de Blic family, the family of Charles' sister, for permission to use the numerous photographs found in this volume.

Finally, I'd like to thank my own community, which has put up with me while I worked on this project and had little time for many of the more usual things that are part of our daily life!...and for the feedback that helped me clarify and hone certain ideas. I am glad to get back to the "ordinary life" that has helped me understand what "Nazareth" is really all about.

Part One

———•◆•———

Understanding the Mind and Heart of Charles de Foucauld

INTRODUCTION

ON THE EVENING OF DECEMBER 1, 1916, Charles de Foucauld was killed in a raid on the *bordj*, or small fort, where he was living alone in Tamanrasset, in the Hoggar region of Algeria. He had been tricked into opening the small door of the *bordj* and was immediately pulled outside, where he was ordered to kneel against a wall with his arms bound behind his back. While some of the insurgents ransacked the *bordj*, a 15-year-old boy held Charles at gunpoint. After some time, two Algerian soldiers, bringing the mail, were spotted approaching on horseback. In the ensuing confusion and panic, the boy guarding Charles pulled the trigger. A single shot behind the ear and the *marabout* (holy man), as he was called, died instantly. The two soldiers were also killed.

———— •◆• ————

Two popular misconceptions exist regarding the life and death of Charles de Foucauld. The first is that he set out to live in the Sahara as a hermit, and the second is that he died a martyr for the faith. Neither of these is based in fact, but both are understandable stereotypes of a priest living alone in the Sahara Desert. We easily conjure up images of the ancient desert monks

3

who fled their cities to seek God in the solitude of the desert wilderness. But Charles de Foucauld did not fit into that, or indeed any, mold.

The truth is that Charles went to the Sahara not to flee from others, but to draw near to a group of people who were considered geographically inaccessible. In the process, his life became intimately bound with theirs. He died a casualty of the violence of World War I, the effects of which reached even those remote corners as vying armies enlisted local tribes in the struggle for power.

Some people who have studied Charles' life and the political situation of the day speculate that the raiders had intended to take him hostage and use him as a pawn in the political upheaval sweeping the land. To the insurgents' way of thinking, eliminating this Frenchman's presence would further weaken the loyalty of those who had sided with the French colonial presence, such as the Tuareg with whom Charles lived, thus leading to greater destabilization in the region.

The *bordj* in which Charles lived had been newly built according to his own design. It was meant to serve as a safe refuge for the poor of Tamanrasset, who did not have the means to flee to the mountains should an attack occur. Within the *bordj's* sturdy walls were a well, provisions, and even some weapons that could be used in self-defense. Charles had just moved there so that everything would be ready in case the people needed to take shelter from the growing threat of violence.

Charles knew the risks of living in Tamanrasset, and he could have protected himself by taking refuge with the military. Likewise, he could have fled with the richer nomads into the mountains rather than remain in such an isolated spot. Although a number of options were available to him, Charles decided to remain in Tamanrasset in solidarity with the people with whom he had shared so much and who had grown to be his friends. This solidarity ultimately cost him his life.

As interesting as the facts immediately surrounding Charles' death may be, the way he died was simply a consequence of a choice. He had made this choice many years before his death, out of love for and in solidarity with another people. He reached beyond the boundaries of culture, race, religion, and language—generally considered to be the barriers separating people from one another—to embrace the "other" as brother and sister. The way he did this and his underlying faith can provide insights for our own living.

——•◆•——

Charles had first visited the Hoggar region of Algeria twelve years before, in 1904. He had prayed a long time over his decision whether to settle in that part of Algeria and where to live once he got there. He considered whether he should settle in a remote area where his prayer and meditation would not be interrupted; where he could be a hermit, alone with the God whose love had so deeply touched his life. Then again, perhaps he should settle on the edge of Tamanrasset; it was a small and isolated hamlet, but he would have contact with the Tuareg nomads of the region. As he wrestled with the question in a written meditation, he imagined Jesus speaking to him:

> It is love which should recollect you in me, not distance from my children. See me in them, and, like me at Nazareth, live near them, lost in God.[1]

From a letter written shortly before his death, we gain further insight into Charles' thinking:

---

1. Diary, April 26, 1904, *Oeuvres Spirituelles* (Paris: Editions du Seuil, 1958), p. 360.

...I believe that there are no other words of the Gospel which have made a deeper impression and transformed my life more than these: "Whatever you do to the least of these little ones, you do to me." If we imagine that these words are those of uncreated Truth and come from the mouth of him who said, "This is my body, this is my blood," with what strength are we impelled to seek and to love Jesus in these little ones, the sinners, and the poor....[2]

Charles stressed the fact that "no other words of the Gospel" had made such an impression on his life as these. He read them in the light of the Eucharist, of Jesus' total gift of himself and abiding presence among us. His meditations were ratified by the way he chose to live out his life in imitation of Jesus' life in Nazareth. Charles' reading of the Gospel, and of the events that life presented, impelled him to make certain choices that altered the course of his life. *Nazareth*, a word charged with many layers of history and meaning for Charles, is one of the keys to understanding his life from 1888 until his death in 1916. Nazareth represented a life of deep intimacy with his beloved brother and Lord Jesus, but it also drew him ever closer to a people with whom he wanted to share that experience of love.

Early Years: A Time of Tears and Confusion

The Viscount Charles Eugène de Foucauld was born on September 15, 1858, in Strasburg, France. He and his only sister, Marie, who was three years younger, were born into the means that came with aristocracy. Charles mentioned very little

---

2. Letter to Louis Massignon, August 1, 1916, *L'aventure de l'amour de Dieu*, Jean François Six (Paris: Editions du Seuil, 1993), p. 210.

about his childhood in his later writings, but remembered his mother as a saintly, gentle woman who taught him to pray. He also remembered going to Mass with his father and grandfather.

When Charles was six years old, his parents tragically died just months apart. Charles and his sister went to live with their paternal grandmother, but this arrangement did not last long. One day, as the children were out walking with their grandmother, a herd of cows overtook them. In her fear that they would be trampled, the woman became so alarmed she suffered a heart attack and died. We know from a letter Charles later wrote how deeply this event affected him. It also became the root of his devotion to Our Lady of Perpetual Help; a small detail, perhaps, but one that affected his spirituality in later life.

> I love Our Lady of Perpetual Help very much because of her title and because of the short prayer which is on the back of her picture and which is so fitting to the situation of our human misery. I also love her because the first time that I saw that image was at my grandmother's deathbed. They had placed that picture of Our Lady on her breast. These are the kinds of things which remain in one's heart.[3]

Having suffered this new loss, the children now went to live with their maternal grandfather, who spoiled the children in an effort to ease their pain. A retired colonel in the French army, Colonel de Morlet was the last in his family's long line of military men—a number of whom had been honored as war heroes.

Six years passed. The Franco-Prussian War broke out, forcing the family twice to evacuate to a safer area. During this time, Charles developed a close relationship with a cousin eight years

---

3. Letter to Dr. Balthazar, January 23, 1891, Archives for the Canonization of Charles de Foucauld.

older than he, Marie Moitessier. Perhaps the relationship provided some needed feminine presence, or maybe her simple and
warm kindness filled a void for Charles. Some have even specu-
lated that the adolescent Charles was in love with her. Whatever
the case, we do know that throughout Charles' later life Marie
would play a very important role: one of support and counsel as
well as deep friendship.

Given the number of losses he experienced early on, it's not
surprising that Charles grew into a troubled young man. While
he never specifically spoke about it, his increasing rootlessness also coincided with his cousin Marie's leaving home to marry
Olivier de Bondy. Although some biographers have made the case
that he became despondent over Marie's departure, Charles never spoke of his feelings. What is certain is that he again lost an
important figure who had lent stability to his life.

Charles loved to read, but his intellectual curiosity and
choice of philosophical works led him away from faith in an age
of religious skepticism and so-called enlightenment. He lost his
bearings and sense of meaning, failing miserably at his school-
work because he never studied and simply did not care. His
grandfather managed to pull enough strings to have him admit-
ted to a military college, where he eventually finished at the bot-
tom of his class.

While Charles was still a student at the military academy his
grandfather died, an event that dealt a final blow to any sense of
stability he may have felt. At nineteen years of age, now with a
sizeable inheritance, Charles began drinking heavily, overeating,
and throwing wild parties; by all standards, he seemed totally
out of control. As he later recalled, "I was self-centered, sacrile-
gious, full of every evil inclination. I had gone wild." He was, in
fact, lost and confused.

> I felt a painful void, an anguish and a sorrow I've never felt
> before or since. This sadness returned each evening as

soon as I found myself alone in my room. I was withdrawn and burdened.... I organized parties, but when they actually took place I had nothing to say and was disgusted.[4]

From Playboy to Explorer

Having graduated, Lieutenant de Foucauld's first tour of duty was in colonial Algeria. There his wild behavior caught up with him. He was dishonorably discharged for insubordination to his commanding officer and for, among other things, parading his mistress, Mimi, around as the Viscountess de Foucauld. Upon Charles' return to France, his family went to court to have a trustee appointed for him, thereby limiting the amount of financial damage he could do to his inheritance. He had been spending enormous amounts of money on a lavish lifestyle, and his trustee now put him on a budget. Charles had been using his wealth to try to fill that "painful void" in his life, which, at the time, he described as a desire for "pleasure."

Just a few months later, Charles learned that the French army was going to see some "real action" in Algeria because of a revolt among some of the tribes. He re-enlisted, promising to abide by military decorum and regulations, and leaving his mistress once and for all.

Charles not only abided by military rules, he proceeded to distinguish himself in the field. He showed himself a real leader among his men, caring for those in his charge even to the point of sharing his meager rations with them. It seemed as if a new Charles de Foucauld were beginning to emerge, one capable of enduring hardship—even thriving in the punishing desert conditions—and of giving himself devotedly for others. He experi-

---

4. Retreat at Nazareth, 1897, *La Dernière Place* (Paris: Nouvelle Cité, 1974), pp. 101–102.

enced great satisfaction in accomplishing the difficult, selfless things of which he was capable, but had never before exerted himself to do. Once the "action" was over, however, Charles resigned his commission "to give free reign to my desire for adventure." He declared that he was not about to while away his life in a garrison somewhere.

Charles' time in Algeria seems to have awakened another side of his character, though he still sought "action" and the pleasure of adventure. He decided that he wanted to explore Morocco, a territory closed to "Christians" (as all French people of the time were considered, though by this time, Charles considered himself agnostic). Several previous expeditions to Morocco had met with disastrous and even fatal results, the attempts having been accurately viewed by Moroccans as part of the French colonial expansion in high gear at the time. But such a dangerous mission spoke to Charles' desire to do something daring, something that no one else had been able to do. He prepared for the journey while living in Algiers, spending up to sixteen hours a day for months on end studying Arabic, Berber, Hebrew, history, and geography, as well as the surveying skills he would need—a far cry from the lazy student of only a few years earlier. He also called on the expertise of some of the most famous men of the day—such as MacCarthy, Maunoir, and Duveyrier—who had a lifetime of experience in exploration.

Charles decided that his best chance to travel safely would be to assume the identity of a poor Russian Jew, a group despised but tolerated in Morocco. Under this guise, no one would be remotely interested in associating with him. For eleven months Charles made his way across Morocco, traveling with a poor Rabbi by the name of Mordecai, whom he had hired to accompany him. (Unbeknownst to Charles, his sister Marie had promised Mordecai a bonus if he brought her brother back alive!) The unlikely pair joined a caravan, with Charles—who carried his notebooks and survey instruments hidden under his robes—separating himself from others to "pray" and thereby make his geographical notations. This extremely risky and difficult trip was rewarded with a prize from the French Geographic Society. The praise was well earned; Charles doubled the existing geographical information about Morocco in the volume he eventually published titled *Reconnaissance au Maroc*.

Ever the adventurer, Charles seemed to be finally pulling himself together and doing "something worthwhile" with his life. His trip had stirred something deep within him. Charles had not spent his entire time in Morocco traveling across sand dunes. He also spent significant amounts of time in towns where he and Mordecai mostly lodged in the Jewish quarter. At other times they stayed in *zaouias*, communities that formed around a particular Muslim *marabout*, or holy man. In these places Charles encountered the mystical forms of Islamic prayer associated with the brotherhoods. He was struck by the sense of the sacred that gave such meaning to the lives of those he met and traveled with and whom he watched at prayer so many times a day. These encounters left him with many questions about the deeper meaning of things. He wrote:

> Islam had a profound effect upon me.... The sight of this faith and these souls living in the continual presence of God helped me to recognize something greater and truer than my own worldly preoccupations.[5]

Charles had put up with privations of every sort during his trip. His life had been threatened on several occasions when people figured out that he was not really a poor Jew. It was thanks to the hospitality of Muslims, who took him under their protection at considerable risk to themselves, that he survived. He

---

5. Letter to Henri de Castries, July 8, 1901, *Lettres à Henri de Castries* (Grasset, 1938), p. 95.

formed lasting friendships with a few people he came to know. When he accepted the prize from the French Geographic Society, Charles spoke of them by name and of the "debt of gratitude" he owed to them. Still, while Charles had accomplished a great deal of scientific work, neither his work nor the acclaim he received from it seemed to fill the emptiness that gnawed at him.

Questions and Conversion: Seeking the Face of God

Back in France, Charles busied himself with writing up reports about his exploration. His family began to pressure him to marry. He actually became engaged at one point, but his family vehemently opposed his choice, feeling that the young woman was an unsuitable match. His cousin Marie finally convinced him to break off the engagement; Charles would later comment that she had "saved" him.

Gradually, as the emptiness in his life gave way to questions, Charles turned to reading philosophy and discussing religion. These discussions were all very rational and intellectual, but they were far from the pointless ones he had engaged in only a few years before. He was truly searching now, going at it the best way he knew how.

The goodness and warmth with which his family had welcomed him back also struck Charles. The example of their faith-filled lives provoked new questions. He loved and respected his family; if they were so good and intelligent, surely what they believed was also worthy of respect. Charles renewed and deepened his relationship with his cousin, Marie de Bondy. He began a strange pilgrimage, irresistibly drawn to visiting churches and praying to a God his mind could not yet accept: "If you exist, let me know it." This preoccupation filled most of the year 1886.

One day in October of that year, not long after his twenty-eighth birthday, Charles approached Father Henri Huvelin in St. Augustine's Church in Paris. Father Huvelin, a noted spiritual director and seminary professor, was a family friend and probably knew some of Charles' story. Charles wanted to discuss religion. Instead, Father Huvelin promptly invited the young man to confess his sins and then sent him to receive Communion. In these two sacraments, Charles experienced the overwhelming mercy and tender love of God. His whole life changed from that moment.

> As soon as I believed there was a God, I knew that I could do nothing else than to live for him alone. My religious vocation dates from the same hour as my faith.[6]

Charles now knew that he wanted to live for God alone, but he had no idea how he was called to do this. It took time for him to sort out many lingering questions. For a while he mingled passages from both the Koran and the Bible in his prayer. His family still hoped to see him marry. None of them, except for his cousin Marie, were aware of the profound change that had taken place in his life. To them he had simply come to his senses and started going back to Church. Despite his encounter with grace, Charles de Foucauld remained his impulsive self, but now given to an excess of another kind. Though he knew nothing about the religious life, and his own was still so unsettled, he expressed the desire to join a religious Order right away. He wanted his choice to reflect the most extreme rupture with everything he had known in his former life and with his newfound fame. He wanted to leave it all and live for God alone. Father Huvelin, who played an important role as Charles' spiritual guide until his death

---

6. Letter to Henri de Castries, August 14, 1901, *Lettres à Henri de Castries*, p. 96.

in 1910, made the young man wait three years. He helped Charles to get his bearings and develop a more solid foundation in the faith. During this time Marie de Bondy was also a great support, and Charles came to consider her as his second, and spiritual, mother.

The Discovery and Call to Nazareth

Two years after Charles' conversion, Father Huvelin suggested that he make a pilgrimage to the Holy Land. This pilgrimage proved to be a decisive moment, one in which the grace of God broke through in a significant way.

Charles arrived in Bethlehem for Christmas of 1888. He was struck by the "incredible humility" of a God who loved us so much as to become one of us. He then proceeded to visit Jerusalem. There, contemplating the cross, Charles realized the depth to which this saving love would go.

> Having spent Christmas 1888 in Bethlehem, having attended midnight Mass and received Holy Communion in that holy Grotto, after a few days I went to Jerusalem. I had felt such an unspeakable sweetness in that Grotto where I could almost hear the voices of Jesus, Mary, and Joseph and where I felt so close to them. And then, alas, after one short hour's walk I was before the dome of the Church of the Holy Sepulcher, Calvary, and the Mount of Olives. Whether I wanted it or not, my thoughts shifted and I found myself at the foot of the cross.[7]

Yet it was Nazareth that made the deepest impression on Charles. There he recognized his own vocation to imitate the life of Jesus, the workman of Nazareth, in his poverty, hiddenness,

---

7. Letter to Father Jerome, December 21, 1896, *Lettres à mes frères de la Trappe* (Paris: Editions du Cerf, 1991), pp. 147–148.

and humility. Charles didn't feel called to imitate Jesus' public life of preaching, but he could see himself living in imitation of what he imagined had been Jesus' life at Nazareth.

Charles saw this imitation in the light of Jesus having taken the "last place" (a theme from a homily Father Huvelin had preached), of his "descent" from heaven and from his equality with God, as we read in St. Paul's letter to the Philippians (2:6–8), to a place of total obscurity. It must be said that Charles, coming from the upper classes of French society and having little concept of the dignity of manual labor, considered any form of manual work a huge "descent." For Charles, the fact that Jesus had been a manual worker meant that he had taken the "last place." From equality with God to manual laborer, "Jesus had so taken the last place that no one has ever been able to take it from him," Father Huvelin had said. And Charles, in his love for Jesus, wanted to imitate him.

Life As a Trappist Monk: Still Searching for Nazareth

Shortly after his pilgrimage to the Holy Land, Charles began a serious discernment process as to which religious community he should enter, using his concept of "Nazareth" as a measuring rod. He finally entered the Trappist Monastery of Our Lady of the Snows in France and asked to be sent to a very poor monastery in Akbès, Syria. "Why did I enter the Trappists? Out of love, out of pure love...."[8] In fact, he left for Akbès after only a few short months—much sooner than a new brother ordinarily would have been sent elsewhere—since, as a member of the army reserve, he could have been called again to active service.

8. Letter to H. Duveyrier, April 24, 1890, *Lettres et Carnets*, ed. Jean François Six (Paris: Editions du Seuil, 1995), p. 26.

Once out of the country, Charles informed the military of his new status and resigned his commission for good. However, his motivation for going so far away was not to avoid a "back door draft." He desired to make the most radical sacrifice he could imagine for Jesus—totally cutting himself off from the world and even from his family, in order to be alone with God. According to his thinking, the only way to live for God alone was to leave everything else behind.

Radical that he was, Charles—now known as Brother Marie-Albéric—wanted not just a poor place, but the *poorest* place. Soon, however, not even the monastery in Akbès, isolated in the mountains and snow coming through the roof of the room where the brothers slept, was poor enough for him. Then at a meeting of Trappists, upon the urging of authorities in Rome, it was decided that the monks should mitigate a few of the most austere practices and even allow a little butter on their vegetables! Charles felt they had stepped onto a slippery slope.... To make matters worse, the monks wanted to build a real road to the monastery, and they put Charles, with his skills as a surveyor, in charge of the project, thereby making him the supervisor of others. Again, this was not the last place that he had been seeking.

It is very likely that nothing would have satisfied his need for austerity and capacity for endurance. As his restlessness increased, Charles worried that he would not find with the Trappists the "Nazareth" he sought. The life kept him from imitating "Jesus, who had taken the last place."

One day Charles was sent to pray at the home of a poor workman who had died. The experience led him to realize that the monastery provided a security that the very poor didn't have, that even he had not had when he traveled in Morocco. He felt sheltered from the concrete poverty of the people, the poverty that Jesus had chosen to live in Nazareth. Also at that time, ethnic Armenian Christians were being massacred throughout the area. As Europeans, the monks were being protected by the same Turkish forces that carried out these atrocities—and with the full knowledge of French government officials. Outraged, Charles wrote to people in France to raise awareness of the situation and to solicit funds to feed the refugees.

On the Sultan's order, nearly 140,000 Christians were massacred in just the last month or so.... The troops in Marach, the closest town to us, killed 4,500 Christians in two days alone. The Europeans have been placed under the protection of the Turkish government, which means that we are safe. They even posted soldiers at our gate to make sure that no one harms us.

It is so painful to be in good standing with those who cut the throats of our brothers. It would be better to suffer with them than to be protected by their persecutors. Shame on Europe. With one word they could have prevented these horrors but did not. It is also true that the outside world knows very little about what goes on here. The Turkish government has paid off the press, giving enormous sums of money to certain newspapers so that they only publish the official press releases. But the governments know what is going on through their embassies and consulates. God will sorely chastise them for such horrible deeds. I am asking you to help us help them, to keep several thousand Christians who managed to escape and take refuge in the mountains to keep from dying of hunger. They are too afraid to leave their hiding places and have absolutely nothing. It is our duty to do without in order to give to them. But no matter what we do, we simply do not have the resources to meet such a need.[9]

9. Letter to R. de Blic, May 3, 1896, *Charles de Foucauld—explorateur au Maroc, ermite au Sahara*, René Bazin (Paris: Nouvelle Cité, 2003), p. 150.

Such events impacted Charles' evolving understanding and longing for "Nazareth." Besides all this, the Trappists had set him on course to study for the priesthood, which again conflicted with his personal vocation to the "last place." He neither desired nor felt worthy of the honor of the priesthood. Instead, Charles began dreaming of founding an Order that would live in the image of his "Nazareth." He deeply wanted to do the will of God, whatever that was, and felt torn. Sharing his feelings with Father Huvelin and with his Trappist superiors, he prayed and waited. The Trappists did what they could to help him through this difficult period, even sending him to Rome to meet with the Abbot General. In all, he remained with the Trappists for seven years before his superiors confirmed his desire to seek "Nazareth" elsewhere.

Hermit in the Holy Land and the Decision for Priesthood

Leaving the Trappists, Charles returned to the Holy Land where he had first heard the call to "Nazareth." Although it was not clear to him what such a call really meant, he was still looking for obscurity in imitation of Jesus. He hired himself out as a handyman to the Poor Clare Nuns in Nazareth, and he lived in a shed in their garden, which he dubbed the Hermitage of Our Lady of Perpetual Help. Actually, Charles was not very "handy." The nuns had taken him in only because Charles' reputation had preceded him and they knew who he was—the Viscount-turned-monk. From time to time the nuns asked him to run errands for them, to paint holy pictures, or to do odd jobs, but mostly he spent enormous amounts of time in prayer, meditation, and reading.

Most of Charles' written meditations on Scripture come from this period. If we have so many of them, it is partly due

The birthplace of Charles de Foucauld, September 15, 1858, in Strasbourg, France.

A portrait taken of Charles when he was two years old.

The Viscount Charles de Foucauld, 1860.

Charles with his mother and younger sister, 1862.

The young schoolboy.

1876, as a military student enrolled at Saint-Cyr Academy. Charles is 18 years old.

Two drawings made by Charles of what he looked like when he traveled through Morocco disguised as a Russian Jew.

Charles in 1889, shortly before joining the Trappists.

The Trappist monastery, Notre-Dames de Neiges, where Charles entered and later took the name Brother Marie-Albéric.

The garden shed in which Charles lived while he worked as a handyman for the Poor Clares.

to Father Huvelin. When Charles told the priest that he had trouble remaining awake during his hours of prayer, Father Huvelin suggested that he write out his meditations as a way to help him focus.

In his prayer Charles experienced times of elation and times of utter dryness, and this comes through in his writings. It also seems that during this period Charles was truly touched by some kind of a mystical experience. It was a deeply graced moment in his life. He deepened his understanding of the Jesus of Scripture and sat in adoration at the feet of his Beloved, allowing the love he met there to reach more deeply into his heart.

We can gain some insight into Charles' thoughts and experience of that time through a letter that he wrote to a certain Brother Jerome, who experienced scruples over spending so much time in retreat while preparing for ordination:

> It is necessary to enter the desert and remain there a while in order to receive the grace of God. It is in the desert that we empty ourselves, that we chase away all that is not God, that we completely empty out the little house of our souls so that God alone may fill it.... It is indispensable.... It is a time of grace.... It is a period through which any soul that wishes to bear fruit must pass. Silence, recollection, and withdrawal from the world are the means God uses to form the inner spirit and establish his reign within us. Intimacy with God.... Conversation between the soul and God in faith, hope, and love.... Later, the soul will bear fruit to the same extent that it has been inwardly formed. If the inner life is non-existent, there will be no fruit despite all the zeal, good intentions, and work. It wants to impart holiness to others but cannot, not having it to give. One can only give that which one possesses. It is in solitude—alone with God alone, in the profound recollection that leaves all behind to live alone

in union with God—that God gives himself completely to
the one who gives himself completely to God.[10]

The flip side to living such a cloistered existence, with little
ordinary activities and conversation for balance, was the absence of
a "reality check." Small wonder that Charles was always coming up
with one fantastic scheme or another, and was even tempted to
return to the Trappists. One of his brainstorms was to buy the
Mount of the Beatitudes, to be ordained, and to live there as a
hermit-priest. In fact, he had become embroiled in a scam that cost
his family no small amount of money, since he had managed to con-
vince them, against their better judgment, to support his idea.
Another project he considered was to support a poor widow—es-
sentially to indenture himself—so that her only son could realize
his "higher calling" to be ordained a priest. Yet another of Charles'
ideas was to act on his earlier desire to found his own Order—the
Hermits of the Sacred Heart of Jesus. He even wrote two versions
of a Rule of Life, begun in Akbès, during the three years he spent
in Nazareth. Father Huvelin considered the very idea "frighten-
ing" and tried to discourage him, clearly telling Charles that he did
not have a gift for leading others in religious life. The priest wise-
ly counseled Charles to stay in Nazareth, hoping that time would
help Charles to sift through his various desires and wild ideas and
reveal what lay at the real core of his vocation.

During this time Charles began to better formulate a concept of "Nazareth" as a way to be a contemplative while sharing
the ordinary, day-to-day life of people by being in close contact
with them. Perhaps the reason Charles had trouble articulating
what "Nazareth" meant to him when he wrote his Rule was because no models for such a form of religious life existed.

---

10. Letter to Father Jerome, May 19, 1898, *Lettres à mes frères de la Trappe*,
pp. 182–183.

Meanwhile, the Poor Clares encouraged Charles to be ordained in the hopes of gaining a resident chaplain for themselves.
Their efforts were partially successful. Charles abruptly returned
to France with ordination in mind, a total reversal from his thinking while he was with the Trappists. He began adapting his concept of "Nazareth" to incorporate the idea of priesthood, which
he no longer considered a position of honor but of service. As a
priest, he would be able to offer Mass and, therefore, make Jesus
more present in the world. Father Huvelin, somewhat stunned
but not against this about-face, helped Charles realize his goal
and put him in touch with the diocese of Viviers, France. Charles
planned to return to the Holy Land as a hermit-priest; but once
again the unpredictability of grace and his response to it led him
elsewhere. As he meditated on what he was undertaking and on
the priesthood of Jesus, something changed.

> My last retreats before diaconate and priesthood showed
> me that my vocation to the life of Nazareth should not
> be lived in the beloved Holy Land, but among those souls
> which are the most sick, the sheep who are the most aban-
> doned. This divine banquet of which I am the minister
> must not be presented to brothers, family, and wealthy
> neighbors, but to the lame, the blind, and to the souls who
> lack priests the most.[11]

Up to this point, Charles' relationship with Christ had largely been a private one, bordering on a "me and Jesus" emphasis
that could have cut him off from the world. A twofold develop-
ment was now taking place that opened the relationship to not
only include others, but also to orient his life toward actively seeking to bring others to know this Jesus, who had so touched his

---

11. Letter to Father Caron, April 8, 1905, *Charles de Foucauld—explorateur
au Maroc, ermite au Sahara*, p. 187.

own heart. While clearly missionary in its own way, his was not a militant evangelistic attitude, but one of a lover needing to include others in the good news of being loved. In his logic, Charles needed to do for others what he would want them to do for him. It never dawned on him that they would not be interested.

Charles completed his studies for the priesthood while living with the Trappists in France, and was ordained on the feast of the Sacred Heart, 1901. From his experience in North Africa, he had a vivid image of those whom he considered to be the furthest away, the most abandoned, and the most in need of a priest. Charles received permission from the Apostolic Prefect of the Sahara to settle in Beni Abbès, Algeria, near the Moroccan border. His hope was to return to Morocco when the political situation would permit. He had a "debt of gratitude" to pay to the people who had not only saved his life, but whose deep faith and spirituality had also played such an important role in his own faith journey.

Beni Abbès, Algeria

Alone in Algeria, Charles began to establish his new way of life. Since the only model of religious life he really knew was a monastic one, he built a small "monastery" of several rooms and a chapel around a courtyard, and marked out his "enclosure" with a row of stones, traces of which can still be seen in the desert. For Charles, the main difference between his monastery and that of the Trappists was that his had an "open enclosure," one where everyone was welcome. During his retreat before ordination, he had also changed the name of the Order he hoped to found from "Hermits" to "Little Brothers" of the Sacred Heart of Jesus, a significant detail that reflects the evolution of how he envisioned his presence. Far from an exclusive "me and Jesus" type of existence, he wanted to "do the greatest good for souls." He wrote: "I want all of the inhabitants—Christian, Muslim, and Jew—to see me as their brother, the universal brother."[12]

Charles envisioned his monastery as a Christian form of the *zaouias* in which he had stayed in Morocco. His monastery quickly became something of a social center, as he gave alms to the poor and became the pastor of the area:

> The fraternity [as he referred to it], which is very quiet at night and between 10:00 A.M. and 3:00 P.M., is a beehive of activity from 5:00 A.M. until 9:00 A.M., and from 4:00 P.M. until 8:00 P.M. I never stop speaking with or seeing people: slaves, the poor, the sick, soldiers, travelers, the curious.... I celebrate holy Mass...before daybreak so as not to be disturbed by the noise and to be able to spend my time of thanksgiving somewhat quietly. But it seems that no matter how early I begin, I am always called away three or four times during my thanksgiving.[13]

Beni Abbès was about as far south as a civilian European could travel in colonial Algeria at the time. Charles' ability to settle there was largely due to his military connections, which could somewhat confuse the issue of Charles' presence among Muslim people if not seen in context. As a former military man from a well-known family, Charles knew people who were able to open doors for him. His reputation as an explorer of Morocco gained him further respect in a very anti-clerical France. He used these connections to gain entrance to a region that would have otherwise been closed to him.

When Charles arrived in Beni Abbès in 1901, he was quickly confronted by the political and social issues affecting the Sahara, the most critical being the manner of French colonial presence.

---

12. Letter to Marie de Bondy, January 7, 1902, *Itinéraire Spirituel de Charles de Foucauld* (Paris: Editions du Seuil, 1958), p. 275.

13. Letter to Marie de Bondy, July 12, 1902, *Lettres à Mme. de Bondy* (Paris: Desclée De Brouwer, 1966), p. 104.

It's important to understand that Charles did not look at the world of his day with twenty-first-century eyes. A man of his own time, he really did think that colonialism, the globalization movement of the day, could be a positive agent of change and for the betterment of other peoples. He felt that the ideals supposedly intrinsic to French society and culture could serve others well, and that the Christian values that were thought to form the basis of that society could only be a blessing to others. Charles was initially very idealistic, but his eyes were quickly opened to reality.

Many of the people he welcomed night and day—he reported receiving as many as 60 to 100 visitors daily—were the very poor or runaway slaves seeking food or help of some kind. While slavery was officially condemned by the French government, local military officials turned a blind eye to it in order to garner the support of powerful, local Algerians who sought to maintain a feudal system. Charles solicited funds to redeem a few slaves, including a young child, whom he named Abd Jesus, and an elderly, blind woman he thought was dying whom he called Marie. These were his only two "converts," his missionary idealism meeting squarely with reality.

But redeeming a few slaves did not address the basic issue of slavery, and his sense of justice cried out for a more fundamental response. Charles began writing letters, both to local officials in Algeria as well as in France, to protest these injustices. By trying to speak on behalf of the voiceless around him, Charles set himself in opposition to the status quo while, at the same time, remaining convinced of the potential good of the colonial system. He was quite aware of the fine line that he was trying to walk, the ambiguity of his situation, and the basic distrust of the Algerian people. Later, as he traveled with a military convoy and spent time in the camps of local nomads, he wrote:

> The local people receive us well, but it is not sincere.
> They give in to the situation. How long will it take for

them to really feel the way that they try to act? Maybe never.... Will they know how to distinguish between soldiers and priests, to see us as servants of God, envoys of peace, universal brothers?[14]

Mostly, he lobbied Church officials in very strong language to intervene in the slavery issue.

We must say—and have the authorities say—"This is not permitted." Woe to you hypocrites, who write on your stamps and elsewhere Liberty, Equality, Fraternity, Human rights, and who attach the shackles of slaves. You falsify the money which bears these words, in condemning people to slave galleys and permitting children to be stolen from their parents and publicly sold. You punish the theft of a chicken and permit that of a person.

We must love our neighbor as our self and do for these poor souls that which we would wish them to do for us, to keep all of those whom God has entrusted to us from perishing. And God has entrusted all the souls of this territory to us. No one is more convinced than I that we must not be mixed up in temporal, government affairs. But we must love justice and hate iniquity. When the government commits grave injustices against those who are to some extent in our charge...we must tell them. We represent justice and truth on this earth and we do not have the right to be "sleeping sentinels," "silent watchdogs" (Is 56:10), or indifferent shepherds.[15]

It was a time of huge political upheaval in France. Many religious Orders had been disbanded by the government, proper-

14. Letter to Marie de Bondy, July 3, 1904, *Charles de Foucauld—explorateur au Maroc, ermite au Sahara*, p. 298.

15. Letter to Dom Martin, February 7, 1902, *Lettres à mes frères*, pp. 276–277.

ties had been seized, and it was feared that high profile interference by the Church in the colonies would jeopardize the Church's precarious position and the real good that was being accomplished, notably through the Fathers and Sisters of Africa (the White Fathers and White Sisters, as they were generally known). Bishop Charles Guérin, the Apostolic Prefect of the Sahara, asked Charles to stop his lobbying which, while well intentioned, was making a lot of noise and causing hostility rather than doing any good. Those who had been in Algeria, and who were quite aware of the problem, were trying to deal with the slavery issue in other ways, which they felt might be more effective. Charles desisted under protest.

Interestingly, in a 1911 letter he wrote almost prophetically:

> Algeria, Tunisia, Morocco, Sudan, the Sahara: What a tremendous empire this will be, provided that we civilize it and bring it into the French mainstream rather than simply content ourselves with holding onto it and exploiting it.... If we ignore the love of neighbor which God, our common Father, has commanded, if we forget the notion of fraternity, which we inscribe on our walls, we will have treated these people not as children, but as something to be exploited. And then the unity which we will have helped to build among them will turn against us and they will throw us into the sea at the first European difficulty.[16]

Charles also had to deal with the disdain and anti-Catholicism of many members of the French military or of those who simply felt that the religious presence was interfering with the colonial agenda. It seems that Charles managed to win the hearts of many who questioned his presence through

---

16. Letter to Fitz James, December 11, 1911, G. Gorrée. *Sur les Traces de Charles de Foucauld* (Lyóns: Editions de la Plus Grande France, 1936), p. 455.

his simple, down-to-earth goodness and holiness. A somewhat suspicious General Lyautey, commander of the local subdivision, passed through Beni Abbès to check out this monk. He knew both Charles' reputation as the famous explorer of Morocco and as a holy man, and he wanted to see Charles for himself. Lyautey later wrote about having been at Mass in Brother Charles' chapel:

> His hermitage was a real hovel! His chapel no more than a miserable hallway with columns, covered with thatch! His altar was just a board! He had an image of Christ painted on cloth hanging over the altar, metal candlesticks! Our feet were in the sand. Well, I have never seen anyone say Mass like Father de Foucauld.... It was one of the most impressive experiences of my life.[17]

And far from being distant in his holiness, Charles felt that laughing and joking were important morale boosters for people living in such austere conditions so far from home (as with the military), and a way to reach out to the local people as well.

The Call of the Hoggar

Just two years after arriving in Beni Abbès, Charles received an invitation from Colonel Henri Laperrine to visit the Hoggar region of southern Algeria, where the Tuareg people lived. Laperrine felt that Charles' presence of friendship and goodness could do more to win the hearts and minds of the people than large detachments of soldiers.

Laperrine lured Charles with the story of a certain Tuareg woman by the name of Taghaichat, who was from a noble family. She had harbored a group of French soldiers wounded in the massacre of the Flatters Mission twenty-two years earlier. The

---

17. Ibid., p. 187.

story of this colonial expedition, decimated by tribes who resisted the French occupation, was well known. Taghaichat had taken the survivors in, protected them from those who wanted to finish them off, cared for them, and helped them to reach safety in Tripoli. Laperrine held her up as an influential woman known for her charity.

On one level, Charles didn't need a lot of convincing to go to the Hoggar. His lingering desire, however spiritual, for adventure—still a part of his personality—and the excess of work and activity in Beni Abbès must have made the prospect tantalizing. In a letter, Charles reported the story to Bishop Guérin. A journal entry from this time reveals Brother Charles' own desire to see someone reach out to Taghaichat, and through her to others: "Isn't this soul ready for the Gospel?"

Bishop Guérin was not so enthusiastic about the idea. Charles felt that the bishop had a subtle, but definite, tendency to push him toward a type of missionary work that he did not consider his vocation to Nazareth. He sensed that the bishop wanted him to carry out traditional types of work that would take him out of his monastery. Charles still felt that "Nazareth" was the life within his cloister. Unless a pressing need of charity called him elsewhere, it meant preaching by his life and not by his words. And yet Charles saw the unexpected invitation that had been extended to him and him alone as a sign that should outweigh his reluctance. He decided to go. On the point of leaving, however, he received news of a massacre of French soldiers near Taghit. There were many wounded and they asked for a priest. Charles left immediately, riding through the night to reach the men. He remained with them for about a month, helping to nurse wounded soldiers back from the brink of death before returning to Beni Abbès. In the meantime, he had missed the convoy heading for southern Algeria. Was this not perhaps another, counter sign? He decided to stay in Beni Abbès.

It was also during this time that he had a visit from Bishop Guérin, a White Father, who was an energetic and prayerful man in his thirties. What a rare pleasure for Charles to have a confrere with whom to pray and share. He longed to have such a companion. After the bishop left, Charles wrote to him:

> For the first time in many years I felt alone Monday evening as I watched you slowly disappear into the shadows. I understood and felt that I was a hermit.... And then I remembered that I have Jesus, and I said, "Jesus, I love you."[18]

The following year, 1904, Charles received a second invitation to travel to the Hoggar. Again there was the uncertainty, the weighing of the pros and cons, the correspondence with Bishop Guérin and Father Huvelin. Was this invitation a call or a temptation? Going out into the desert with a military convoy hardly amounted to a "desert experience" of solitude and prayer. Charles finally saw it as a call to ministry; after all, he was the only priest who was being given such an opportunity. He decided to go.

During that first journey, Charles traveled with a military detachment made up in large part of Algerian (Muslim) soldiers and a few French officers. Laperrine traveled with the convoy for the first five months of the trip. In many ways these were Charles' first steps outside of the cloister and very important in his evolving notion of Nazareth.

Charles traveled with the detachment for over a year—mostly on foot out of a sense of humility—and he was glad for the chance to get a feel for the country and the people. The convoy stopped in oases and villages where he met people and began learning the rudiments of the Tamahaq language. He wrote of

---

18. Letter to Bishop Guérin, June 3, 1903, *Correspondances Sahariennes* (Paris: Editions du Cerf, 1998), p. 185.

meeting Taghaichat, whose story had so influenced the direction of his life, even if his idealized image of what she represented had little to do with reality.

It was apparent that the people barely tolerated the French occupation in the region, and several Tuareg chiefs refused to allow the party to camp in their villages. Laperrine was keen to have Charles meet Moussa Ag Amastâne, one of the local Tuareg chiefs. If the *marabout* were to settle in the Hoggar and live there alone, he would need approval from Moussa, and Laperrine wanted to see Charles settle there. But they missed Moussa by a few weeks. During this time Charles began translating the Gospel into Tamahaq.

Charles faced another dilemma as he pondered whether to settle in the Hoggar. As tempting as the prospect was for him, he had achieved something of his dream in Beni Abbès, and he kept hoping for others to join him there. To leave now would mean giving up what he had built so far, not just the physical building, but also part of his dream. Most likely there would be no other brothers if he went further south, since access to these areas, as well as finding anyone willing to go there, would be nearly impossible. It also meant giving up the possibility of celebrating Mass. Church law of the day did not permit a priest to celebrate the Eucharist alone; at least in Beni Abbès he had the possibility of a server.

> Is it better to stay in the Hoggar without being able to celebrate Holy Mass, or to celebrate and not to go? I have often asked myself the same question. Before, I would have sacrificed everything else to have the celebration of Mass. But something must be wrong with this reasoning. Ever since the time of the Apostles, the greatest saints sometimes sacrificed the possibility of this celebration in favor of spiritual works of mercy. It is good to stay here alone. Even if one isn't able to do a great deal, it is worth-

while becoming a part of the scenery; one is so approachable and so "very small."[19]

Still Charles questioned. He would have to spend months traveling—a contradiction, in his mind, to his life as a monk. Finally, settling in the Hoggar would mean giving up his dream of going to Morocco. After returning to Beni Abbès at the end of that year, Charles convinced himself that he was called to stay in his cloister at Beni Abbès. However, he used the time normally dedicated to manual work, as his Rule required, to instead recopy his notes concerning Tamahaq from the previous year's travels. He would send these to Bishop Guérin in the hopes that they would be helpful for someone else's future mission among the Tuareg.

Soon another opportunity to go to the Hoggar presented itself, but this time it was a question not of visiting but of settling there. Again the opportunity was being offered to him and to him alone. Charles looked for some confirmation of the will of God. He knew his own impulsive nature and didn't want to act simply according to his own desires. After much communication, Bishop Guérin wired him to "be inclined to accept the suggestion to go." Both Bishop Guérin and Father Huvelin had come to recognize that these deep, persistent urgings might well be the work of the Spirit in Charles, as well as an opportunity for the Church to be present in the Hoggar through him.

So it was that in 1905 Charles returned to the Hoggar, with the idea of spending his time between there and Beni Abbès, and still clinging to the hope of having a companion. He had repeatedly asked Bishop Guérin if he knew of anyone who might be a potential little brother. On a trip north to see the bishop, he started back with a young man named Michel. But after only a few weeks Charles sent him home, deeming that he did not have the "stuff" necessary for such an austere life. Then again, who could

19. Letter to Bishop Guérin, July 2, 1907, *Correspondances Sahariennes*, 1998, p. 527.

have really kept up with Charles? Brother Michel, in fact, later
became a Carthusian monk, one of the most austere religious
Orders of the day.

The convoy to the Hoggar was led by Captain Jean Marie
Dinaux and included a geographer, a geologist, and a journalist,
as well as several officers, Tuareg interpreters, and the usual military detachment. Charles finally met Moussa, the *Amenokal*
(chief) of the Hoggar, who had signed a peace treaty with the
French. There was some concern about how the meeting would
go, but the two men came to a real respect for and, eventually,
friendship with one another. Charles wrote his first impressions
of their meeting:

> Moussa, their chief, is a remarkable man. He is intelligent,
> with a broad vision of things, God-fearing, very pious. He
> is an honest man who truly desires peace and the common
> good as he understands it.... He is thirty-five years old, has
> lived a just life until now, and is very much loved through-
> out the country.... If he continues in this way we can ex-
> pect much from him, through him, and for him.[20]

The convoy spent several weeks with Moussa in the Hoggar
and Charles decided to settle alone in the village of Tamanrasset,
sight unseen, which was in Moussa's territory. Moussa welcomed
his presence, possibly recognizing the potential benefits of collaborating with the French.

Nazareth in Tamanrasset

In Tamanrasset, Charles built a house that was just one long
room, about six feet wide and twenty feet long, divided into three

---

20. Letter to Bishop Guérin, July 13, 1905, *Correspondances Sahariennes*,
p. 357.

parts. Even this reflected the evolution of his thought regarding Nazareth. When he first sought it, he had entered the Trappist monastery in order to cut himself off from the world and to live for God alone. Then there had been the little shed within the Poor Clares' enclosure. In Beni Abbès he had built a small "monastery" while waiting for the brothers he hoped would join him. But it had been an enclosure with a mission to be a presence to others and, therefore, a place of welcome.

Now there was no longer even the pretense of an enclosure. The whole desert was his enclosure. There would be no great "works," but a ministry of presence to the people; no worrying about observance of the Rule that he had written, but use of it only as a general guide. He imagined Jesus telling him, "It is love which should recollect you in me, not distance from my children. See me in them, and, like me at Nazareth, live near them, lost in God."[21]

For years "Nazareth" had meant "descent"—to be always poorer, to be hidden—and Charles had always expressed it in extreme language. It had also meant distancing himself from others. The shift in his understanding of "Nazareth" that had begun at his ordination and continued at Beni Abbès, now became an even greater sense of going to what seemed to him one of the remotest corners of the earth in order to be with those who were so far away. It was an orientation toward and not away from others. In fact, this was what Charles discovered the descent of the Incarnation to be all about. Jesus came to be one of us, to share our ordinary life, and, through his very oneness with us, to be Emmanuel, the presence of God among us. This concept is so important, because all too often Charles is portrayed as a hermit living alone in the desert in the style of the ancient desert

---

21. Diary, April 26, 1904, *Oeuvres Spirituelles*, p. 360.

monks. While he had a natural attraction to and love of solitude, the love of Jesus that he encountered in that solitude became an ever deeper call to reach out to those for whom Jesus came. It was a springboard to a new way of being a contemplative.

> I have chosen Tamanrasset, a village of twenty campfires in the heart of the Hoggar Mountains and of the Dag Rali, the major tribe of the area, far from any sizable village. I don't think that there will ever be a military post here, nor telegraph, nor Europeans, nor mission in the foreseeable future. I have chosen to settle in this obscure little corner, asking Jesus to bless this place where I hope to have, as my only example, his life at Nazareth.[22]

Charles' beginnings in Tamanrasset were very austere. Although he lived alone and the nearest military post was miles away, people were suspicious of his presence and kept a distance. He had decided not to repeat his experience in Beni Abbès, not to become a social-service center that would take a whole group of brothers to run. Instead, he wanted to enter into relationship with people and simply to share any surplus that he had. As a result, his presence did not initially attract many visitors. He didn't even see any soldiers for months on end; mail was a rare event.

Charles threw himself into working on a Tuareg-French dictionary and lexicon. He learned a precious lesson from a linguist by the name of Motylinsky, who spent a few months with Charles when he had first settled in Tamanrasset. Charles had invited Motylinski, a scholar of the Arabic and Berber languages and professor at the University in Constantine, to come to Tamanrasset. The two had known each other from Charles' military stint in

---

22. *Carnets de Tamanrasset*, August 11, 1905 (Paris: Nouvelle Cité, 1986), p. 48.

Algeria. Motylinski taught Charles to listen to the people rather than translate what he wanted to communicate to them. For two months the old friends worked together, collaborating on the beginnings of a Tuareg-French dictionary. Their work together ended prematurely with the death of Motylinski less than a year later. Although Charles, realizing the many deficiencies in the work that had been cut short, would completely rework all of Motylinski's notes over the years, he always insisted that it, as well as work entirely his own, be published under Motylinski's name. He wanted no credit or glory for any of it.

Charles had begun learning Tamahaq during his travels; now he began also noting customs and poetry, sometimes working over ten hours a day. He started paying local women to recite poetry and tell him stories, and he hired a man by the name of Ben Messis, and later another, Ba Hammou, to be his teachers. Eventually Charles recorded 6,000 verses of poetry. It was a labor of love that he undertook with the same attention to detail and energy with which he had explored Morocco. He drew detailed pictures of everything from musical instruments to the way the women braided their hair. This new approach was much more than simply a change of technique. Charles realized how indispensable such things were in order to understand the soul of the people. In paying careful attention to these details, his own soul was opened to truly meet the Tuareg. It led him to a deeper appreciation of who God had created them to be.

Charles believed that he was doing work that would prepare the way for others who might come after him. The more he studied and discovered the depth and intricacies of the Tamahaq language, the more he realized how inadequate his translation of the Gospel was and he abandoned it. There was no rush. He knew that it was not the right time for direct evangelization and that premature attempts to do so would merely push people away.

Charles didn't have the language to name what we today call a ministry of presence. It didn't exist in any explicit form in his day. But he put it this way:

> My apostolate must be one of goodness. On seeing me they must say, "If this man is good, his religion must be good." If they ask me why I am good, I must answer, "Because I am the servant of one who is so much better than I. If only you knew how good my Master, Jesus, is." I want to be good enough so that they will say, "If the servant is like this, how must the Master be."[23]

Charles was clearly still focused on being a missionary presence in some sense, although his understanding of exactly how to live this out was steadily evolving and becoming clearer. A military doctor who had met Charles in Tamanrasset recalled a conversation with him about his presence among the Tuareg. When the doctor asked Brother Charles what he hoped to accomplish, this was his answer:

> I am not here in order to convert the Tuareg people at once, but to try to understand them.... I am sure that the Good Lord will welcome into heaven all those who have been good and honest without them having to be Roman Catholic. You are Protestant, T. has no religious faith at all, the Tuareg are Muslim. I am convinced that God will welcome all of us if we deserve it.[24]

This seems an amazing and radical statement in an age when the Catholic Church taught that there was no salvation outside of the Church. It shows us just how far Brother Charles' thinking had evolved over the years in the face of concrete situations and the God-given goodness of people. Although it was the de-

---

23. Ibid., 1909, pp. 188–189.

24. Leon Lehureau, *Au Sahara avec le Père de Foucauld* (Paris: Editions St. Paul, 1946), p. 115.

sire of his heart that others would come to know Jesus as he knew
him, and at times he felt that his failure must be due to his lack
of holiness, Charles managed not to impose himself on others and
he did not equate missionary success with the numbers of Baptisms
he might perform. In fact, his so-called missionary presence was
not only a failure in terms of conversions, but Moussa became
more fervent in his own faith, wanting to develop Tamanrasset into an Islamic center. The people even prayed for Charles' conversion to their faith, so that he, too, could go to heaven.

A significant event in Charles' life occurred during the winter of 1907–08, two years after his arrival in Tamanrasset. He had
begun to know some of the people. They had been watching him
and were growing more comfortable with him. As winter drew
on, the drought conditions in the area worsened and Brother
Charles shared all of his provisions to help ease the people's
hunger. He had chosen to live in this isolated region, far from the
European community, in solidarity with these people; now he experienced the consequences of that choice in his own flesh. He
wrote to ask his friend, Laperrine, to send him a few things. He
described the situation to his cousin:

> This has been a hard year for the country. There has been
> no rain these past seventeen months. It means total famine
> in a country that depends on milk, where the poor prac-
> tically only have milk. The goats are as dry as the earth,
> and the people as dry as the goats....[25]

Then he fell sick, probably from scurvy.

> I was quite ill these last days. I don't know what it is, some-
> thing with the heart, I think; no cough nor chest pain. The
> least effort makes me so short of breath that I faint. For
> a day or two I thought it was the end.[26]

---

25. Letter to Marie de Bondy, July 17, 1907, *Lettres à Mme. de Bondy*, p. 160.
26. Ibid., January 26, 1908, p. 166.

Besides the experience of physical famine, Charles also suffered a spiritual famine. In the midst of the drought, Christmas came and went, and he still had no permission to celebrate the Eucharist alone. For a time he thought he had authorization to reserve the Blessed Sacrament, but he learned that he had been mistaken. So Charles found himself without even that Presence in which he had always found such solace.

> Christmas. No Mass this night for the first time in twenty-one years. May his will be done.... Until the last moment I kept hoping that someone would come. But no one came, not a Christian traveler, soldier, nor permission to celebrate alone. I haven't had any mail in over three months.[27]

To grasp the significance of this statement it is important to understand the place the Eucharist held in Charles de Foucauld's life. It was central from the day of his conversion until the day of his death. He never lost his hunger and joy for the Real Presence. His whole life was somehow centered around the Eucharist and adoration of the Blessed Sacrament, and he believed that the presence of a tabernacle in the Hoggar had a real and sanctifying effect.

Charles was at his lowest point, physically as well as spiritually. He felt himself broken and a failure. Previously no matter how poor he was, he had always been the one who had something to give to others. True to missionary customs of the day, he felt that he should never receive anything from the people, never be beholden to them. Now, for the first time in his life, he had nothing left to give.

Charles was now the one in need, and the Tuareg responded by scouring the countryside looking for a little bit of milk to

27. Ibid., December 25, 1907, pp. 164–165.

nurse him back to health. Their sense of the sacredness of the duty of hospitality moved them to care for this foreigner. Charles truly owed them his life. Weakness brought about a level of relationship that would not have been possible without this reciprocity. It was a conversion for him in terms of his own inner life—of accepting his weakness and need—and one that further transformed his theories about mission into a relationship of friendship. He later wrote:

> The Tuareg of the area trust me more and more, old friends become closer, new friendships form. I do what I can and I try to show my love. When the situation permits, I speak of natural religion, God's commandments and love, of union with his will, and of love of neighbor....[28]

Finally, on January 31, 1908, the supplies from Laperrine arrived, along with a letter giving him permission from Rome to celebrate the Eucharist alone. Charles was overwhelmed with joy. Although he could now celebrate the Eucharist, it would be six more years before he received permission to reserve the Blessed Sacrament, and he never had the conditions necessary for exposition and "adoration."

The Final Years

From 1905 until his death in 1916, Charles spent most of his time in Tamanrasset. At one point he thought of spending long periods in the even more remote region of the Assekrem, hoping for greater contact with some of the other nomadic groups. He had his famous hermitage built high in those mountains and went there with Ba Hammou to work on the Tuareg

---

28. Letter to Fr. Voillard, July 12, 1912, *Correspondances Sahariennes*, p. 863.

dictionary. The two men spent five months there, until Brother Charles finally ceded to Ba Hammou's objections to the strenuous living conditions and they went back to Tamanrasset. In reality, they met very few nomads in that remote and arid region, and he never returned there.

Charles continued working on his dictionary in Tamanrasset until shortly before his death. For a man with no formal training in linguistics, he accomplished a phenomenal task. The dictionary is a four-volume, hand-written encyclopedia that goes into the minute details of definitions and grammar, as well as containing a collection of cultural and social practices. The collections of poetry and prose relate historical and cultural events, transliterated as well as translated into more fluent French.

For Charles these were works lovingly undertaken to "prepare the way for others," but they remain works with tremendous objective value. The Tuareg stood on the verge of losing some of their identity through contact with both the Arabs and the French, who were making their presence increasingly felt. Such a collection was a treasure for a people whose written language was used only for short notes and whose history was largely oral.

One can only imagine that someone like Charles also drew a certain satisfaction from accomplishing such a task, while at the same time drawing him closer to the people. The Tuareg teased that he spoke their language better than they did. Charles was known for his ready laughter and large, welcoming smile (even at the expense of showing his bad teeth), as he grew increasingly "little and approachable." People said that he never kept them waiting when they came to see him, as other Europeans did. The French soldiers remarked with some astonishment that Charles seemed genuinely at ease among the Tuareg, even preferring their company to that of his compatriots. Charles wrote to Henri de Castries:

> I spent the entire year, 1912, here in the hamlet of
> Tamanrasset. The company of the Tuareg is such a com-

fort to me. I can't tell you how good they are to me, what upright souls I have found among them. One or two are true friends—such a rare and precious thing anywhere.[29]

It is interesting to note that the torment Charles had previously suffered regarding how and where to live out his vocation disappeared once he settled in Tamanrasset. It seems that he not only found his "Nazareth," but also became more truly himself, more fully human.

Charles gradually realized that there would be no religious brothers or sisters to follow him, and so, in the last years of his life, he decided to work toward the establishment of a lay association. During a trip to France, he managed to interest a few people in being part of this group. From his own experience he knew that lay people could often be present in situations where religious and clergy were excluded. He used Priscilla and Aquila, whom we meet in the Acts of the Apostles, as models of a form of lay evangelization through presence.

Louis Massignon, a young Frenchman and student of Islam who had undergone a powerful conversion experience of his own, had been on the verge of joining Brother Charles for several years. The relationship between the two men was one of friendship as well as spiritual direction. After deciding to marry instead of joining Charles, Massignon became very involved with this lay group and spearheaded the efforts to establish the association that Brother Charles had hoped to found. Massignon, who went on to become a well-known Islamic scholar, also founded a group known as *Badaliya*, with one of its goals being Christian-Muslim relations.

In 1921, five years after Charles' death, the well-known French writer, René Bazin, published the first biography of Charles de Foucauld. It planted a seed that blossomed into the

---

29. Letter to Henri de Castries, Jan. 8, 1913, *Lettres à Henri de Castries*, p. 196.

founding of several religious Orders of Little Brothers and Little Sisters inspired by Charles' spirituality. They began by trying to follow the Rule he had written but quickly realized that not only had Charles not followed it in any practical sense, it was also totally unlivable. Fortunately, his meditations, and especially his letters, provided a more realistic glimpse into the "Nazareth" for which he was reaching.

———•·———

Brother Charles had often meditated on death and martyrdom. In the idealism of his youth he had desired to die as a martyr in order to be like Jesus, who gave his life for others. In later years, Charles saw so much that needed to be done and so many people whom he felt God had entrusted to his care, he said that he no longer desired martyrdom. Yet, he was very conscious of the fact that his solidarity with the Tuareg people at that time and place could lead to his death. Years before in Nazareth, in one of his meditations on the passion, he had written:

> No matter why they kill us, if in our hearts we welcome an unjust and cruel death as a blessed gift from your hand; if we give you thanks for such a sweet grace, for such a blessed imitation of your own end; if we offer it to you in willing sacrifice without resistance in obedience to your word...and your example...then, no matter why they kill us, we will die in pure love and our death will be a sweet-smelling sacrifice. And if it isn't martyrdom in the strict sense of the word and in the eyes of men, it will be so in your eyes and it will be a very perfect image of your own death.... If we have not shed our blood for our faith we will have offered it with our whole heart, handed over out of love for you.[30]

---

30. Meditation on the Passion, Nazareth, 1897, *En vue de Dieu Seul* (Paris: Nouvelle Cité, 1973), pp. 217–218.

Charles de Foucauld was killed on the first Friday of December. The Church traditionally observes the first Friday of each month in honor of the Sacred Heart to remind us of the depths of God's love for us. Charles had painted a large image of the Sacred Heart, which he hung above the altar to remind him of that love—the same love that he found in the Eucharist and that was so central to his whole spirituality: the Word made flesh, broken and shared for us.

Charles de Foucauld wanted to conform his life to that of Jesus. "Do this in memory of me" was a way of living as well as dying. His whole life became Eucharistic. Paul Embareck, an eye-witness of his death, said that during the raid Charles never uttered a word but knelt in the sand in silence. Several weeks later, when soldiers arrived, after learning of his death, they found the Blessed Sacrament discarded in the sand among the last pages of his dictionary, in many ways a symbol of his love for the Tuareg put into practice, the symbol of a life given out of love.

Part Two

———•◆•———

Praying with Charles de Foucauld

INTRODUCTION

PRAYER CAN BE DESCRIBED AS THE easiest thing in the world: a simple conversation with God; sitting in God's presence and opening one's heart to the love of God; taking the time to turn one's gaze toward God in love. What could be simpler? But anyone who has tried to pray regularly over a period of time also knows how hard it can be to remain in that presence and welcome God's grace into one's life. We often talk about our prayer and our relationship with God with friends and spiritual directors, looking for support and encouragement for our journey.

These next chapters invite you to pray with Charles de Foucauld. They are meant to offer a few pearls from the experience of someone who spent a great deal of time in prayer, who learned to deal with the same struggles that we all face—albeit in a different context than most of ours. Charles' is a very human, and humanizing, pathway. The humanity we share is the common ground that makes one person's journey of faith a source of insight for others.

Each of the following chapters explores different aspects of Charles' journey of faith, and then offers questions or suggestions that might be helpful in orienting your own prayer. The themes covered certainly do not exhaust what Charles has to share with us;

neither are they assignments to be completed! If a particular theme or suggestion doesn't "speak" to you, pass over it. The goal is simply to meet Jesus along the way, to know and love him more deeply.

While Charles' prayer was very Jesus-centered, three times a day he prayed the *Veni Creator*, a prayer that asks the grace of God's Spirit to touch every aspect of our life. Before continuing, you might take a moment to ask for that same grace.

Veni Creator (Come, Holy Spirit)

Come, Holy Spirit, Creator, come
From your bright heavenly throne.
Come, take possession of our souls,
and make them all your own!

You who are called the Paraclete,
Best gift of God above,
The living spring, the living fire,
Sweet unction and true love!

You who are sevenfold in your grace,
Finger of God's right hand,
God's promise, teaching little ones
To speak and understand.

O guide our minds with your blest light,
With love our hearts inflame,
and with your strength which ne'er decays
Confirm our mortal frame.

Far from us drive our deadly foe;
True peace unto us bring;
And from all perils lead us safe
Beneath your sacred wing.

Through you may we the Father know,
Through you, the eternal Son,
And you, the Spirit of them both,
Thrice-blessed three in one.

All glory to the Father be,
And to his risen Son,
The like to you, great Paraclete,
While endless ages run. Amen.

Charles visited his sister and her family for the first time in ten years
after he returned to France to be ordained in September 1900. Here
he is pictured with his nephew, Charles de Blic.

Portrait taken in Beni Abbès, Algeria, in 1902. Charles later explains that he wears a heart on his habit "so that I remember God and men and women and love them."

The house Charles built while in Beni Abbès, with stones marking his "enclosure."

Brother Charles with a three-year-old boy whom he redeemed from slavery and named Abd Jesus. The boy was
one of only two people ever baptized by Charles (1902).

Interior of the chapel the soldiers helped to build in Beni Abbès.

At Beni Abbès with Abd Jesus and Captain Susbielle (1902–1903).

Tent used for celebrating Mass while Charles traveled to the Hoggar.

Tamanrasset, May 1912.

Temporary shelter (*zriba*) where Charles lived while building the house in Tamanrasset.

Charles' house in Tamanrasset.

The hermitage in Assekrem where Charles spent five months studying Tamahaq (1911).

Visiting in a Tuareg camp while traveling in the Hoggar along with a French officer.

Charles with a group of Tuareg men (1908–1909).

In Tamanrasset (1907).

With a young Tuareg by the name of Ouksem Ag Chikkat (1907).
In 1913 Brother Charles brought him to France on a visit home.

Photo taken around 1911–1913.

The *bordj* built by Charles and the people of Tamanrasset.

Aerial view taken several years after Brother Charles' death.

Last known photo: 1915 or 1916.

1

Finding a Home in Jesus

"Remember your compassion and love, O Lord;
for they are ages old. Remember no more the
sins of my youth; remember me only in the
light of your love" (Ps 25:7).

To understand the story of Charles' conversion and the
image of God's love that inhabited him, it is necessary first to understand his background and early influences on his life. The
death of his grandfather seems to have been the final event in a
succession of losses that pushed Charles over the edge. "In one
stroke my family, my home, my peace of mind have been taken
from me. I will never find it again."[31] In such a state of mental an-
guish, his behavior deteriorated as he tried to numb himself to
the pain and confusion that overwhelmed him. As he wrote:

> ...It was night, there was nothing left. I could no longer
> see either God or others. There was only myself.... I was
> totally self-centered; mired in darkness. Even my most

---

31. Letter to Gabriel Tourdes, February 5, 1878, *Lettres à un Ami de Lycée*
(Paris: Nouvelle Cité, 1982), p. 73.

worldly companions had lost all esteem for me. I disgusted and revolted them. I was more like a pig than a man, rolling in the muck![32]

————·•·————

Charles' behavior changed considerably both while he prepared for his Moroccan expedition and through what he called the circumstances of the trip, which, among other things, imposed chastity on him. But he was still in a state of personal crisis when he returned to France. Through the notes he made during his trip, we begin to see another Charles emerge: not just the intrepid explorer, but a man who had been touched and somehow shaken at the core of his being. It is striking to read his words:

> In this profound calm, in the midst of this other-worldly nature, I had my first real taste of the Sahara. In the contemplation of the starlit nights one understands the belief of the Arabs in a mysterious night—*leila el gedr*, they call it—when the heavens open and angels descend to earth and the sea's waters become sweet; then the whole of inanimate nature bows down to worship its Creator.[33]

————·•·————

What did he know of worship? Having witnessed the Moroccans' deep Islamic faith, Charles was filled with questions and a gnawing hunger that his success and the accompanying acclaim could not satisfy. A year and a half passed between the end of his expedition in Morocco and the day he asked to speak with Father Huvelin at St. Augustine's Church. During that time, as

32. Retreat at Nazareth, *La Dernière Place* (Paris: Nouvelle Cité, 1974), p. 94.
33. Charles de Foucauld, *Reconnaissance au Maroc* (Paris: Editions d' Aujourd'hui), p. 164.

much as Charles had engaged his mind to appease his hunger, his reason had also blocked his path with endless intellectual arguments.

Father Huvelin cut through all of this when he invited Charles to receive the sacrament of Reconciliation. It was an invitation for Charles to open his heart and meet a God whom he could trust, who would never let him down or abandon him, and, most of all, who accepted and loved him despite his sinfulness. It was a powerfully healing and overwhelming experience for Charles.

> Your first grace, which I now see as the first glimmer of my conversion, was to let me know famine.... You had the goodness to let me suffer from material difficulties. You let me know spiritual famine...and then, when I turned so timidly toward you and prayed that strange prayer, "If you exist, let me know it," with what tenderness you ran to embrace me.[34]

In a meditation Charles later wrote about the gospel story of the return of the Prodigal Son, we can glimpse what this experience must have meant for him:

> How good is the father of the prodigal son! But you are a thousand times more tender than he. You have done a thousand times more for me than he did for his son! You are so good, my Lord and my God! Thank you, thank you, thank you, forever thank you! The prodigal child was received without punishment, reproach, or dragging up the past. He was received with such ineffable goodness, with kisses, the finest robe, and a ring. Not only received, but sought after by this blessed Father and brought back by him from foreign lands.[35]

---

34. *Imitation du Bien Aimé* (Paris: Nouvelle Cité, 1997), pp. 78–79.
35. Ibid., p. 79.

God always invites us to come home, often speaking to us precisely through our loneliness and hunger. God respects the limits of our woundedness and knows how to wait, while always offering grace. So many times we understand this only afterward. We may never experience such a dramatic "return" as did Charles, but all of us have known the separation, hurt, or shame that our poor choices have brought on us, as well as God's healing forgiveness and the grace of reconciliation. Perhaps even now there are areas of our lives where we have yet to "come home."

Charles' experience of conversion helped him to reach out to others in their sense of shame and confusion. He knew, through the "ineffable goodness" with which his family had welcomed him back, that God uses others to draw us. Many of the French soldiers who would later know him attested to Charles' goodness and to the kindness with which he looked on them, never condescending but caring. These were hardened legionnaires not "weekend warriors," yet they felt drawn to this "little priest" who won them over.

Charles' compassion is also very poignantly expressed in his correspondence over the years with the young Louis Massignon, who suffered the throes of his own spiritual crises and feelings of guilt. Charles wrote to him:

> No, past faults do not frighten me. Human beings cannot forgive them because they are not in a position to give back lost purity. God forgives and wipes away the slightest stain, giving back the fullest and first beauty.[36]

> Don't be surprised about the misery which remains despite good will and grace. The misery will always be there. You will be all the more aware of it the greater your good

---

36. Letter to Louis Massignon, December 3, 1909, *L'aventure de l'amour de Dieu*, p. 68.

will and the more abundant the grace. Be patient, take it easy with yourself, humble yourself in front of your failings without getting discouraged. Each time that you become aware of your faults, may it bring to birth a double act of humility and love, trust and hope....[37]

Peace, trust, hope. Don't be so hard on yourself. The miseries of our soul are like a mire within, and we should often humble ourselves about them, but we should not always keep our eyes fixed on them. We must fix our eyes also, and more surely, on the Beloved, on that beauty and infinite love with which we are loved.... When we love, we forget about ourselves and think of the One we love. Thinking that we are always unworthy of love is not loving....[38]

Charles was captivated by the love of Jesus, and he spoke from the experience of love. He wanted to live in imitation of his Beloved. How better to imitate Jesus than to focus all of one's being on the Beloved, just as Jesus had lived in such deep union with his Father? In this manner, Charles took the focus off himself and turned it toward God, the only One in whom healing and wholeness could be found.

[Jesus] grew in wisdom, age, and grace. As he grew in age and wisdom, an abundance of divine inner graces showed themselves more and more.... May it be the same with us. As we grow older, may the grace that we received in Baptism and those received through the sacraments be seen more and more clearly in our actions. This grace is the gift of God, given with growing abundance to the faithful soul. May each day of our lives see us growing in

37. Letter to Louis Massignon, May 29, 1914, *L'aventure de l'amour de Dieu*, p. 162.

38. Ibid., May 1, 1912, p. 128.

wisdom and grace. Let us cry and be humble if this is not the case, especially if by some misfortune we should err. But do not become discouraged. If we stop or take a step backwards, let it make us more humble, less sure of ourselves. Let it make us more vigilant, indulgent, and full of goodness for others. May we be more gentle, humble, respectful, and brotherly with our neighbor. May we be repentant, aware of our own wretchedness and ungratefulness but always with trust in God, always sure of God's love, always loving God more tenderly and thankfully, in spite of our misery. After every setback, tell him, like St. Peter, "Lord, you know that I love you."[39]

Focusing our prayer

- Find that quiet place that helps you to pray. Enter that "space," both the physical area as well as the place within yourself where you meet God, with reverence. Do you know that you are beloved and that God continually calls you home? Take some time to simply savor this knowledge. Give thanks for the grace of God that draws you with "chords of love" (cf. Hos 11:4).

- The prodigal father recognized his son from a long way off. His son was his flesh and blood. Do you believe that you are made in the image of God and that God sees that you are "very good"? Read the story of creation in the first chapter of Genesis or take time with Psalm 139. Read the passages slowly, with the eye of your heart.

---

39. Meditation on the Gospel of Luke, *Oeuvres Spirituelles*, p. 335.

- Can you recall particular moments when you knew forgiveness in your life, when you were forgiven or were able to reach beyond your hurt to forgive another? What happened in those moments that allowed you to open your heart in such a way?

- Charles wrote about the story of his conversion in letters to two friends and also as a retreat exercise in Nazareth. Is there a "story of return" that you might write?

- Brother Charles spoke of how instrumental in his own journey were the welcome and love of his family. Who has been instrumental in your journey? What was it about this person's presence that made a difference to you? What does your experience of the tender mercy and love of God mean for your relationships with others?

- Are you aware of the ways in which you block the transforming love of God in your life? Name them.

- God always takes the first step—as well as the second, the third, and the fourth steps—toward us. Eventually, however, we must also take a step toward "home," without which God can only stand there and wait. Is there a "step" that you need to take right now? What is it?

2

RECEIVE THE GOSPEL

"Indeed, the word of God is living and effective, sharper than any two-edged sword, penetrating even between the soul and spirit, joints and marrow, and able to discern reflections and thoughts of the heart" (Heb 4:12).

FROM THE TIME OF HIS CONVERSION, Charles de Foucauld looked to the Gospel for answers to his questions about life. He did so during a period when the Church discouraged lay people from reading the Bible, because lack of education regarding Scripture made its possible misinterpretation a concern. Under the guidance of Father Huvelin, however, Charles discovered Scripture as a precious meeting place with Jesus. He nourished his faith at the table of the Word, and he looked within its pages for understanding and guidance throughout his life.

The first major question Charles faced after his conversion was what he should do regarding his future. He didn't have to look far for an answer. He wrote, "The Gospel showed me that the first commandment is to love God with one's whole heart and that everything must be wrapped in love."[40]

During his years with the Trappists, Charles copied the entire text of the four Gospels into a small notebook that he carried everywhere with him. Before leaving for Nazareth, he began to recopy the same texts in Arabic. Although he thought of himself as a monk who would have limited contact with others, he still wanted to pray these texts in the local language as a sign of his connectedness with those among whom he would live.

From his various writings an image emerges of someone immersed in meditation of the Gospel. Charles met his Beloved in those pages as much as in the Eucharist. His constant reading and re-reading of Scripture helped him to confront his own limited and narrow ideas and images. Scripture held such importance for him that, when he wrote his Rule of Life for the Little Brothers, he began each of the forty chapters with texts from the Gospels. And outlining the daily schedule for the community, Charles wrote:

> Each morning we begin with meditation of the holy Gospel, that is, the words and examples of our Lord. After this hour of meditation, every other hour of the day must be spent by entering more deeply into these teachings that we received upon awakening, and especially to applying them.[41]

Meditation on the words and deeds of Jesus rooted Charles more firmly not only in God's love for him, but also in a vision of the Reign of God. Meditation for Charles was not a private affair, but served as an instrument for transforming how we see life, whether we live within a cloister or among other people. In Beni Abbès, for instance, Charles continually referred to the Gospel in his fight against slavery. He saw the Gospel as an active force

---

40. Letter to Henri de Castries, August 14, 1901, *Lettres à Henri de Castries*, p. 97.

41. *Reglements et Directoire* (Paris: Nouvelle Cité, 1995), p. 35.

for justice. "Whatever you do to the least of these little ones, you do it to me" (Mt 25:40).

Today we have over 2,000 transcribed pages from Charles de Foucauld's meditations on Scripture—focused mainly on the Gospels—and another 700 meditations on the liturgical feasts, in which he continually returns to the words of Jesus. Most of these come from his time in Nazareth, when Charles used writing as a way to help him focus. The style of his meditations reflects the style of the day, and Charles was certainly a man of his time. Similarly, our meditation will reflect the concerns and influences of our own day and age. Yet if we look to Charles for insight on how to live our relationship with Jesus, it is precisely because Charles allowed the Gospel to challenge and pull him out of himself and his own narrow ideas. He read the Gospels from where he stood, at various times and in different circumstances, just as we read the Gospel from our own context. Charles came to understand that he needed to live his relationship with Jesus while actively engaged with the world to which he belonged.

Charles also wrote his meditations at particular stages in his life. He continued to grow in his relationship with God and in his understanding of what his call meant. Certain themes that had seemed important to Charles in Nazareth, he no longer mentioned in later writings, while he continued to develop other ideas throughout his life. We can imagine that if Charles were to reread today some of his writings from 1898, he might make some revisions, especially if he knew they were to be published! Charles' writings were intimate conversations with his Beloved, and he never intended many of them for the public. Others he may have written with his future community in mind.

> Our whole lives, no matter how silent or public—whether the life of Nazareth, the life in the desert, or the public life— must preach the Gospel from the rooftops. All that we are, our every action, our entire life must breathe Jesus, must

proclaim that we belong to Jesus, must give an image of a gospel life. Our entire being must be a living witness, a reflection of Jesus, a perfume of Jesus, something that shouts "Jesus," that reveals Jesus and shines as an image of Jesus.[42]

Charles read other sources besides Scripture, especially the writings of Teresa of Avila and John of the Cross, and even recommended such spiritual reading to his friends. He found in these saints wisdom and encouragement for his own journey. But he was very clear about the prominence that must be given to the Gospel:

Receive the Gospel. It is by the Gospel that we shall be judged, not by any other book or any spiritual master, not by any doctor or saint, but by the Gospel of Jesus, by the words of Jesus, the examples of Jesus, the counsels and teachings of Jesus.[43]

When Charles first entered the Trappists, he cut off contact with most people, believing he needed to do so in order to live for God alone. It was not long before he revised his way of thinking. He decided it was more important to renew contact with his family and friends, so that those relationships would be mutually supportive on the road to loving God.

Charles' correspondence grew over the years to include a wide variety of people. In one of many letters to Louis Massignon, Charles offered the following advice:

Find some time to read a few verses of the Gospel every day, in such a way that over a certain period of time you will have read the whole Gospel. After the reading, meditate for a few minutes, either mentally or in writing, on the teachings contained in the reading. You must seek to be thoroughly filled with the Spirit of Jesus in reading and

---

42. *La Bonté de Dieu* (Paris, Nouvelle Cité, 1996), p. 285.
43. *Imitation du Bien Aimé*, p. 204.

re-reading, meditating on his words and examples over
and over again without ceasing. May it be to our souls like
the steady dripping of water on a stone.[44]

Even in times of dryness and darkness, Charles found the
means to continue to nourish his faith through meditation on the
Scriptures. It is said that he insisted on the sanctuary lamp being placed in such a way as to allow its light to shine not only
on the tabernacle, but also on an open Bible. Both were his food.
He read the Gospel as though he were sitting at the feet of the
Beloved, listening to Jesus speak.

Focusing our prayer

• The practice of a meditative reading of Scripture is known as
Lectio Divina. Take some time to sit quietly, knowing that as
you read the Gospel, Jesus is speaking to you and wants you
to "have life in his name." The words of the Gospels were
spoken to the simple people of Jesus' day, and they continue
to speak to our hearts today "if we have ears to hear." Praying
the Scriptures requires training the ear of our heart to hear
what Jesus has to say to us today. It means allowing the words
of the Gospel to so transform our lives that we become living Gospels for others.

• Consider Charles' advice to his friend, Louis Massignon, cited above. Read a few verses of the Gospel every day, in such
a way as to read the whole Gospel over the course of some
time. But take only a few verses each day, reading them slowly. There is no deadline to be met; there is only Jesus. Reread
the verses and let the Spirit of Jesus speak to you through
them. What is God saying to you in the context of your life?

---

44. Letter to Louis Massignon, *L'aventure de l'amour de Dieu*, p. 166.

- Before the proclamation of the Gospel, it has long been customary to sign oneself with a small cross on the forehead, the lips, and the heart, while praying, "May the words of the Gospel be in my mind, on my lips, and in my heart...." Before reading the text for the day, try this or some other gesture that may help you to slow down and realize that you are on "sacred ground." Invite the Word to dwell deeply within you. The Church proposes for us particular Scripture passages in the Liturgy of the Word proclaimed at daily Mass. When we pray with these readings, we are not alone; we pray in communion with the whole community of believers around the world.

- Read a passage from the Gospel first thing in the morning. Go over it slowly several times—even reading it aloud, if that helps—allowing the words to sink in. Take some time to let those words find a home in you. "If you make my word your home, you will indeed be my disciples. You shall know the truth and the truth shall make you free" (Jn 8:31–32). Is there a word or a phrase that strikes you? Let it "roll around" inside your heart; savor it as one savors good wine. How does it "taste"? At the end of your meditation, read the passage through once again.

  —During the day, try to recall the word that you heard in the morning. You might be waiting for a bus or driving, doing dishes or some other activity. It doesn't always have to be "prayer time" for you to engage in such reflection. All of our moments can become prayer.

  —Does that word look different in the light of the day's activity? How so?

  —Return to the same passage at the end of the day. Reread your day in its light. Give thanks.

- Sometimes when we sit down to "meditate" it is hard to concentrate. Charles began to write out his meditations not as an exercise of objective observation, but as the record of a running dialogue with Jesus. He called it a "familiar conversation with the Beloved." Is there such a conversation with Jesus that you might write?

- Is there a specific text of the Gospel that has had a significant impact on your life and influenced your actions? What was going on in your life at the time? How has this text stayed with you? How has your understanding of its implications changed you? Write about it.

- Charles was moved to draw several large tapestries of Gospel stories, as well as the Stations of the Cross, to express and support his prayer. Is there something that you might do with a text that is important to you and that would make it present in your daily life to remind you of the Jesus whom you met at that important time and place?

- Consider praying the Gospels regularly with a small group of people as a way to nourish your understanding of the Scriptures and to root your reflections in the day-to-day reality in which you are called to build the Reign of God.

3

THE PRESENCE OF JESUS

"The Lord Jesus, on the night he was handed over, took bread, and after he had given thanks, broke it and said, 'This is my body that is for you. Do this in remembrance of me'"
(1 Cor 11:24).

FROM THE MOMENT OF CHARLES' CONVERSION (when Father Huvelin sent him directly from the confessional to receive Holy Communion) until his death, his prayer was rooted in the mystery of the Eucharist. His understanding of the Eucharist as the presence of Jesus was the lens through which he gazed upon the love and goodness of God. Charles immersed himself in this mystery, and it was there that he discovered himself to be more and more a "beloved son." His understanding of the Eucharist was also the lens which eventually brought into focus Charles' place and role as one called to share God's love with others. But this transformation didn't happen overnight.

Charles lived at a time when devotion to the Eucharist flourished and yet frequent reception of Communion was discouraged, because approaching the altar regularly seemed presumptuous.

Instead, Eucharistic adoration came to hold a place of great importance in the prayer life of ordinary Catholics. In his wisdom, and contrary to the practice of the day, Father Huvelin recognized that reception of Holy Communion was not a right one earned through one's efforts to be worthy. Rather, through participation in the Eucharist we are gradually drawn more deeply into the mystery of God's immense love for us, and we are made holy, configured to the image of Jesus. Father Huvelin, therefore, encouraged Charles to receive the sacraments frequently. This practice nourished in him a deep love for the Eucharist and became a focal point of his prayer. Later in his letters, Charles advised others who desired to grow in their spiritual life to do the same.

Charles was deeply drawn to Eucharistic adoration as to a long meditation and "communion" with Jesus. It was a way of simply spending time with the Beloved and of entering more deeply into the mystery of Jesus' love. During Charles' time at Nazareth, in which he wrote so many meditations, we glimpse the intimacy such prayer held for him. Beyond certain expressions that may seem outdated today, we hear the language of the mystics:

> My Lord Jesus, you are there, in the holy Eucharist. You are just a few feet away from me in the Tabernacle.... You are so near, my God, my Savior, my Jesus, my Brother.[45]

> He is not far from me, this Being who is so perfect, this Being who is all Being, who is the only true Being, who is all beauty, goodness, love, wisdom, knowledge, intelligence.... You, my God, you who are all Perfection, all Beauty, all Truth, infinite and essential Love, you are in me, you are all around me.... You completely fill me..., there is no part of my body that you do not fill, and around me, you are closer to me than the air through which I move.... My God, give me the continual knowledge of

---

45. Retreat at Nazareth, November 7, 1897, *La Dernière Place*, p. 81.

your presence...and at the same time that awesome love that one feels in the presence of the one who is so passionately loved. We remain transfixed before the Beloved without being able to take our eyes away.[46]

It is important to note that Charles' prayer before the Eucharist was not a closed affair between him and Jesus. His love of Jesus compelled him to want to be like him, and in some way reach out to others as Jesus had. Prayer before the Eucharist was both the place where Charles contemplated Jesus' sacrifice on the cross and where he experienced a deep communion, through Jesus, with all humanity. Charles realized that the same one who said, "Whatever you do to the least of these little ones..." was the one who also said, "This is my body, this is my blood," and, "Do this in remembrance of me."

While Charles was still with the Trappists in Akbès, he had an interesting reflection regarding the thought of starting his own Order. It was not a major theme in his life, but it gives us a hint of the flavor of his spirituality and the direction in which he was headed. He wrote that in his Order the life of prayer would be much simpler than the complicated Latin liturgies of his day, which ordinary people couldn't understand. He imagined liturgies in the local language, with long periods of silent adoration that he felt would help people who did not have a formal education—who perhaps didn't even know how to read—to pray. In this sense, the practice of Eucharistic adoration for Charles was really a prayer of the poor and for the poor, its only prerequisite being faith in the mystery that is open to all.

The idea also reflected Charles' own experience of prayer. Being a form of prayer with few "props"—it involved simply remaining silent in the presence of Jesus—Eucharistic adoration helped to strip away the illusions that Charles had of himself. His

---

46. Ibid., November 5, 1897, p. 41.

prayer led him to touch his own poverty in a way that opened his heart so that Jesus could dwell there more deeply. It led him to a growing sense of adoration in the broadest understanding of that word: to an attitude of praise.

Reading Charles' meditations on prayer, one may have the impression that he lived in a state of continual ecstasy. This is far from the case. In his prayer, Charles experienced darkness as well as light.

> Aridity and darkness. Everything is painful, even telling Jesus that I love him. I must hold fast to the life of faith. If only I could feel that Jesus loves me, but he never tells me so....[47]

> In order to teach us the value of your presence, to make us more fervent and humble and to help us to want to seek you, you often leave us in times of darkness and dryness.... Prayer, Office, meditation, Holy Communion—it all seems so heavy, so difficult; even telling you that we love you.... We painfully feel our own misery, the chill within our hearts. It seems as though there is a great abyss between us, and that you look on us with severity. We wonder where we are and where we are going, and it seems as though we are sinking in quicksand, unable to free ourselves. But, my God, you are so good! You call to us, "Find yourself in me," and you throw us a solid anchor to which we can attach our joy in such a way that nothing can ever take it away from us, not even the gates of hell.[48]

---

47. Letter to Louis Massignon, June 6, 1897, *Voyageur dans la Nuit* (Paris: Nouvelle Cité, 1979), p. 32.

48. Meditation on Psalm 2, *Meditations sur les psaumes* (Paris: Nouvelle Cité, 1980), p. 44.

Eucharistic theology of the time emphasized the supreme value of the physical Presence of the Blessed Sacrament. Charles believed that in some way the presence of the Blessed Sacrament alone would sanctify persons and places, even in the lives of those who were unaware of or had no faith in the sacrament. We can understand how this theology "fit" with Charles' desire to return to North Africa. In his role as priest, he would bring the "banquet" to those who were far-off through the consecration of the Eucharist in a land that did not have this "Presence."

In connection with this theology, one Gospel image that fascinated Charles was the Visitation (cf. Lk 1:39–56). In this passage, Mary, who has just conceived Jesus, goes to visit her elderly cousin, Elizabeth, who is pregnant with John the Baptist. By carrying Jesus "invisibly present" within her, Mary was, in her own way, reaching out to another and contributing to the sanctification of the world. This was how Charles came to understand his vocation to priesthood during the retreat before his ordination. As a minister of the Eucharist, he felt it would be his mission to establish a tabernacle in far-off lands without other priests, so that Jesus could be present there.

When he went to Algeria, Charles saw the Visitation as an image of the Eucharistic presence silently radiating in a land that didn't know Jesus. Charles didn't consider it important to use words to preach about that presence, especially among people who were not Christian. But by establishing the presence of the Eucharist he could contribute to the sanctification of the world. The Visitation image was so important to him that he drew a large picture of it on a cloth and hung it in his chapel.

So Charles faced a real dilemma when he considered moving to Tamanrasset. He was authorized neither to celebrate Mass alone nor to reserve the Blessed Sacrament under those conditions. Up until this time, he had placed so much value on the physical presence of the Eucharist in his own life and as a sanctifying presence in the world. As he struggled over what to do, Charles ultimately decided that "something must be wrong with this reasoning." He concluded that even if he had to give up the Eucharist, it was good for him to be present in the Hoggar; that living alone in Tamanrasset would make him "approachable and so 'very small.'" Such vulnerability reflects a theology of the Eucharist that sees Jesus handing over his life—not only at his death, but from his birth—into human hands. Now Charles had only his life to serve as that radiating presence. To the extent that he was able to welcome Jesus into his life, he became the means by which Jesus would be present in the world.

Antoine Chatelard, a Little Brother of Jesus who has spent years studying the writings and life of Brother Charles, has referred to this movement as one from "exposition of the Blessed Sacrament" to living a life that allows one's very self to be "exposed" in the image of Jesus' gift of self. This is a powerful image of Charles gradually being transformed into what he had so long contemplated, of his life becoming "eucharistic."

Through the quality of the relationships that he formed with the Tuareg, and through his reaching out to be present to them, Charles also discovered the face of God. He would not have had the vocabulary to express it in these words, but the sacrament of presence became flesh through this communion of true and life-giving friendship.

Beyond our attempts to describe Charles' theology of Eucharist, there is the simple fact that Charles developed a profound attitude of adoration that permeated his whole life. He cultivated a true humility that knows one receives everything from God as a gift. Just like the Muslim people among whom he lived and through whom he received the first glimmers of faith, he learned to bow in adoration before the greatness of God. He discovered that he could remain before the Lord wrapped in silence, finding healing and peace, strength and grace.

Many theological discussions today seem to put the Eucharist as a meal celebrated in community at odds with the Eucharistic presence as a focus for prayer and adoration. Unfortunately, too often there arises a polarization of "camps" rather than a mutual enrichment and appreciation of insight. For Brother Charles no opposition existed between such under-standings; there was one continuum of prayer and praise. He en-tered deeply into the signs and symbols of our faith so that they would support his prayer. The Eucharist for Charles was the sacrament of the "presence" of Jesus among us, a sacrament that did not "stop" at the altar but that transforms all of our rela-tionships.

Adoration of the Blessed Sacrament is a form of prayer that many people, inspired by Charles' life, find to be a source of grace. In adoration, we focus the eyes of our hearts on a partic-ular moment so full of meaning that we need to take the time to let it sink in. It's like pausing in freeze-frame on a mystery of grace. We do this all the time with other events in our lives. We see a photo and are instantly transported to that time and place, remembering who was there and what happened. This "sacred remembering" is the core of our Eucharistic celebrations. We don't "stop" at the end of the Mass, but are sent from the table to live eucharistic lives. Prayer before the Blessed Sacrament is simply a way of taking time to savor the mystery. It may or may not be something familiar to and comfortable for you. It may not be a form of prayer that "speaks" to you. Then again, it may be-come a means to help you to focus your prayer.

Focusing our prayer

- Our liturgy has long made use of certain bodily gestures to express its prayer. You may want to begin a time of adora-tion by kneeling or bowing, prostrating yourself or simply standing to express your reverence. There may be some lingering smell of incense. There may be candles to mark this place as holy.

- You might consciously make the sign of the cross. The mystery of the Eucharist into which you enter is the mystery of Jesus' life, death, and resurrection. We bring with us the "crosses," the joys, or even the boredom that touch our lives; and we look for confirmation and rest, strength and understanding, healing and resurrection.

- There may be days when the only prayer we are capable of is to bring our bodily selves before the Body of Christ. In our flesh, we bear the effects of life. We do not so much reflect on what we are living as we simply present ourselves before Jesus. In a certain sense, the events of life make us who we are at a particular moment in time. And we don't come alone. We bring with us the people whose lives are bound to ours, not so much in a manner of active intercession as in the solidarity that leaves its mark on our flesh and in our hearts. Those events and relationships make us who we are as we sit in the presence of the Lord. Jesus gives us grace to become who and whose we are called to be. Our physical presence *is* our act of intercession.

- Allow silence to envelope you. Don't be afraid to remain in the silence for whatever length of time feels right to you; just linger with the Beloved. Allow him to welcome and love you.

- How has your participation in the Eucharist changed the way you live? What does it mean to you to live "in memory of him"?

4

INTO YOUR HANDS...

"The message of the Cross is foolishness to those who are perishing, but to us who are being saved it is the power of God" (1 Cor 1:17).

PERHAPS CHARLES DE FOUCAULD is best known for the Prayer of Abandon. Contrary to what one might expect, this prayer was not a spiritual testament written by Charles at the end of his life, nor did he use it as part of his daily prayer. As popularly known, the prayer is an excerpt from a longer meditation Charles wrote while with the Trappists and is part of a series of written reflections on the passion. In this prayer, Charles imagines the crucified, dying Jesus speaking to his Father.

As with any prayer that one might imagine coming from Jesus, it reveals much about Charles' own relationship with God. It is an especially intimate and poignant prayer since he never meant others to read it. This prayer was simply the fruit of his meditation. When he wrote it, he was experiencing a time of darkness. Charles was following the Trappist way of life, but struggling with it and questioning his presence there. He was confused and restless. He deeply wanted to live the will of God, but how does someone know what is God's will? He felt great uncertainty about the path ahead.

In the process of trying to discern whether to leave the Trappists, Charles shared his questions and doubts, his fears and dreams with his religious superiors and with Father Huvelin. He placed the final decision in their hands and then waited—a common practice at the time. Had he not vowed obedience as an act of inner freedom? Who was he to say he knew the will of God better than another did? In the big scheme of things, don't we too often discover the face of God in surprising ways we would not have chosen? But this act of surrender was hard for Charles to make.

What enabled Charles to exercise such obedience was his faith in God and the trust born of that faith. These were not abstract concepts for Charles, but experiences of love coming from having met the person of Jesus. Charles also trusted the wisdom and care of those he felt were in a position to guide him. Most of all, he believed that in creating us, God has instilled in each of us an inner strength capable of seeing us through whatever life might throw at us. If only he could tap into that strength....

He meditated on the sacrifice of Abraham found in chapter 22 of Genesis:

> Before such an act of obedience, which implies such faith
> and proves so much love, it is better to keep silent than
> to speak. Let us not speak. Let us admire and pray.... To
> love you is to obey you with promptness and faith in situations that shipwreck the heart and turn our spirits upside down, that upset all of our plans and ideas. To love
> is to sacrifice to your will immediately and absolutely all
> that is dearest to us.... To love is to trade all that seems
> good and to embrace what is painful out of love for the
> Lord.... It is what you so marvelously do in rising at once
> in the night to go and sacrifice your son, St. Abraham. It
> is what you will do, O Son of God, in coming from heav-

en to live such a life on this earth and to die such a death!
My Lord and my God, help me to do it also, according
to your holy will....[49]

We might be tempted to skip over the concept of obedience.
It is so tempting to do only what we want to do or have control
over. But doesn't life at times call all of us to an obedience we
would rather avoid? It might be obedience in our job, to the
friendships that make us a human community, or simply to the
unexpected and uncontrollable events of life. At times commit-
ments can require tremendous sacrifice of us, and the nature of
sacrifice is that it is hard.

Charles lived abandonment into the hands of God at other
moments of his life as well. We hear echoes of his prayer of abandon in many of his writings and letters. As time wore on and no
followers joined him, Charles felt alone; he experienced the
weight of years, his diminishing energy, and a sense of fruitless-
ness regarding all he had hoped to do. The illusions and dreams
of his youth dissipated with age. His acceptance of weakness and
vulnerability certainly opened a precious door to the Tuareg people that he could not have imagined. But to receive this grace and
others, Charles had to embrace many "deaths," both great and
small. He had to let go of illusions about himself and others, and
this was no easier for Charles than it is for us.

In 1910, for example, Charles lost three friends through
death: Father Huvelin, who had been sick for some time; Bishop
Guérin, who died unexpectedly of typhoid; and an officer by the
name of Lacroix. How difficult it must have been for him to lose
people whom he loved, and whose friendship told him something
about himself. Humanly speaking, we all feel bereaved by such
tremendous losses, no matter how deep our faith.

---

49. Meditation, *Qui peut résistera Dieu* (Paris: Nouvelle Cité, 1980), pp.
64–65.

And yet we are called to go on.

To understand the Prayer of Abandon[50] from Charles' per-
spective, one has to remember first that his prayer was, for the
most part, very Jesus-centered, the fruit of his deep, personal relationship with Jesus. There was nothing abstract about it. He often pictured Jesus sitting in the same room with him. Charles
watched, listened, and spoke with Jesus, and he "reacted" to what
he imagined with compassion and empathy.

In the Prayer of Abandon, Charles pictures Jesus on the
cross. He introduced the meditation with these words:

> It is the last prayer of our Master, of our Beloved...may
> it be ours...may it not only be the prayer of our last mo-
> ment but that of all our moments.

Father,
I abandon myself into your hands.
Do with me what you will.
Whatever you may do, I thank you.
I am ready for all; I accept all.
Let only your will be done in me
and in all your creatures.
I wish no more than this, O Lord.
Into your hands I commend my soul.
I offer it to you with all the love of my heart,
for I love you, Lord, and so need to give myself,
to surrender myself into your hands
without reserve and with boundless confidence,
for you are my Father.

---

50. Integral text from which this excerpt is taken is found in *Ecrits Spirituels*
(Gigord, 1923), p. 29.

Charles visualizes Jesus praying to the One whom he calls "Abba, Father." His is not a prayer of hardened resignation but a prayer of love. It is the expression of an abandonment of which only love is capable, the abandonment of throwing oneself into the arms of the Beloved. It trusts the Beloved to be there, despite all evidence to the contrary. It is the declaration of a love that defies the power of death. It proclaims a love capable of trust, a trust in the power of love even in the face of annihilation. Jesus—and Charles—believe that love will have the last word.

The Prayer of Abandon is the prayer of the cross. Jesus no longer prays for the cup to pass him by or even for the strength to drink from it. That was yesterday, and so much has happened since. Jesus is dying now and there is no escape. His strength is quickly ebbing. The only choice left at this hour is how Jesus will live his death. How will he deal with it? He could revolt in the face of its injustice, for no death has ever been more unjust. No one has ever been as innocent. He could become embittered by the jeers and mocking. He could turn to hardened resignation. But Charles shows us a Jesus who chooses to live this moment with a kind of love difficult for us to grasp or imagine. Jesus turns to his Father and finds refuge by plunging into the intimacy of their relationship, "with all the love of my heart." He offers his life with thanksgiving, desiring not only to accomplish the will of God in the world, but also to receive it into his life.

Charles also shows us a Jesus who seems to be alone. It is no longer the moment of the "Our Father." Jesus is facing the deepest solitude, a solitude which we must all ultimately face. It is precisely through his aloneness at this moment that Jesus expresses his great solidarity with us. Death is the threshold where each of us is alone, no matter how many people surround us. Jesus is literally at the point of losing himself, and he chooses to lose himself in the Father. "For you are my Father." It is the abandon of love.

Possibly one of the greatest obstacles to our embracing this prayer with Charles and Jesus is our wounded trust. We will pray it differently according to our own experiences. The brokenness of our world deeply affects our ability, and even our desire, to trust. If the most fortunate among us can think of so many reasons to be cautious, what of those who have been deeply wounded? Who of us has not been betrayed at one time or another?

Focusing our prayer

- Spend some time of prayer before the cross of Jesus, before his wounds and brokenness. What are the wounds and broken places in your life? Perhaps you are deeply affected by the woundedness of another. Lay this at the foot of the cross. Read the Prayer of Abandon again, slowly.

- Take a few moments to consider how you trust. What are the obstacles to your trust—hurts, fears, and resentments? What happens when you bring these obstacles into the intimacy of your relationship with God? Can you remember a time when you were able to trust in the face of difficulty? Where did this strength come from?

- Where do you find refuge when the going gets rough? In whom or in what do you place your trust? Can you take a few moments to sit quietly and "commend" yourself into the hands of God? What happens when you do this?

- What attitude do you want to nurture within your heart in the face of pain, sorrow, or personal hurt? How do you know that Jesus is with you?

- One of the things that trust allows us to do is to wait. Waiting can be so hard and frustrating. Learning to wait well in the small things of life can help us for the hard waiting: when we feel powerless, when there is nothing we can do, when no one can "fix" a situation for us. We want to avoid pain by breaking the tension created by waiting. Surely Jesus wanted the passion to be over with, too. But he accepted the time it had to take to get to the "other side." In learning how to wait, we open the way for something to be born within us. Something comes to term in us that is otherwise immature or poorly developed if we rush. Recall a time when waiting bore unexpected fruit in your life. How did you manage the tension that waiting created? What were its fruits? Where was God?

•   Is there a "Prayer of Abandon" that you might write?

EPILOGUE

SOME YEARS AGO I WAS ASKED to share about Charles de Foucauld's life with a group of priests. At the end, one of them said something to the effect of "That's all very interesting, but what does it have to do with us today?" He really wanted to know. Actually, I could relate well to his comment. I had never found Brother Charles an easy person to connect with.

In the years since, as I have read and tried to write about Charles' life, I have been forced to ask myself the same question. I think that there are different layers of answers, some of which may appeal to different people.

On one level, there was the *"marabout,"* someone whom everyone—Christian and Muslim alike—recognized as a man of God not because they watched him praying for long hours of the day and night, but because they witnessed the fruit of that prayer: his down-to-earth goodness, his kindness, his openness to others, his joy. They sensed that he looked at them with love—a love that he had experienced in Jesus, a love that he knew Jesus had for them, too.

Brother Charles' experience of Jesus and his reading of the Gospel continually took him beyond his preconceived ideas. He called on the Spirit of God, asking to be led in the ways of the

Gospel. Among other things, he moved from an idealized conception of "giving his life to God" through radical, personal poverty, to understanding what it meant to give his life by concretely standing with and sharing the life of the poor, as Jesus had done in Nazareth.

I also discovered that Brother Charles was far from being a plaster saint. It helped to know just how much he struggled with faith and prayer and life—a fellow traveler along the journey. It encourages me to see that through his faithfulness to his relationship with God and to the journey, he became more human as he became more holy, more settled and at peace with himself and with the world around him. Fortunately, that peace did not depend upon some elusive image of "success," which he never found.

On another level, there is this man who discovered "Presence" as a model for mission in an Islamic world. The relationship with Islam is one of the critical issues facing not only the Church, but also our global community today. How are we going to work this out? How are we going to find a path of respect with people who call God Allah, or Adonai, or Shiva, or any of the many names by which we call God in our quest to find life's meaning? Charles de Foucauld found a way through his understanding of God's deep love for all people. He called this Nazareth—that simple meeting place of the ordinary where he believed God chose to dwell, where God took flesh and learned to be human, too; where, in taking our flesh, Jesus helped us to recognize the common humanity that calls us together in love. We believe that through his flesh Jesus put enmity to death. Those can seem like such big words, such grand theories. In reality, it is through the flesh of our daily lives that we are called to continue his mission and to reach for communion.

To answer that priest's question, I think that Charles de Foucauld has all of this and more to say to us today. He learned how to give an "account of the hope that was within him," hope rooted in his faith in Jesus of Nazareth. It is a hope that our world needs today, and it is a model that is within the grasp of each one of us, wherever we are called to live our Nazareths.

Appendix

————— •◆• —————

LETTER TO HENRI
DE CASTRIES

Brother Charles tells the story of his conversion in three existing texts. One is in a letter written in 1892 to H. Duveyrier, an unbeliever who cannot grasp the reason for Charles' choosing to become a religious brother and professing vows at the Trappist Monastery. The second is a meditation he wrote during a retreat in Nazareth in 1897.

In the third text, cited in full here, Charles writes to a friend by the name of Henri de Castries. Although a Catholic, Castries was struggling with issues of faith because of his own study of Islam. Writing on August 14, 1901, Brother Charles was in France having just been ordained a priest. It is touching to read these words addressed to a friend who was struggling with faith just as Charles himself had struggled many years before.

————— •◆• —————

August 14, 1901

My dear friend,

You were telling me that your faith has been shaken.... Let me say that when one loves truth as much as you do, and when one has all the means for knowing it, one always finds it. And so in my deep affection for you I don't worry about you.... Let me speak simply. I am a monk, living only for God, trying to love others for his sake with all the ardor that is mine. They are his image, the work of his hands, his children, his beloved, made to participate eternally in the Godhead. They have been redeemed by the blood of Jesus. I cannot be united with him, who is un-created and infinite love, without loving with all my heart according to his word, "Love one another. By this they will know that you are my disciples." I cannot speak with you or think about you without ardently desiring for you the one thing that I de-sire for myself: God—God, known, loved, and served now and forever.

Forgive me if I speak so intimately. Or rather, I do not ask you to forgive because I am sure that you understand and ap-prove. "Allah Akbar." God is great, greater than anything that we could name. He alone, after all, is deserving of our thoughts and words. If we speak, if you tire of reading all that I write, and if I break the silence of the cloister in order to write, it is that we would both come to better know and serve him. Anything that doesn't lead us to that—to better know and serve God—is a waste of time.

Let me begin by my confession. Your faith has only been shaken. Alas, mine was completely dead for years. For twelve years I lived without any faith at all. Nothing could be proved to me. The fact that such diverse religions are all followed with equal faith seemed to condemn them all. Least of all the religion of my childhood seemed illogical with its 1 = 3 of which I could not make any sense. Islam seemed quite attractive by its very simplicity: simplicity of dogma, hierarchy, and morality. But I clearly saw that it had no divine foundation and that truth was not to be found there. And the philosophers are all in disagreement. I spent twelve years without denying or believing anything, despairing of ever finding the truth, not even believing in God since none of the proofs of God seemed convincing enough.... I was living as one lives when the last spark of faith is extinguished.... What miracle of the infinite Mercy of God brought me back from so far away? I can only attribute it to one thing—the infinite goodness of him who said: *"quoniam bonus, quoniam in saeculum misericordia eus"* (For he is good, everlasting is his love—Ps 106/105) and his Almighty Power.

While I was in Paris to publish the account of my trip through Morocco, I found myself among people who were very intelligent, virtuous, and Christian. I said to myself—excuse my way of thinking aloud—that maybe this religion was not so absurd. At the same time, I was being strongly urged on by an inner grace. I started going to church even though I still had no faith. It was the only place I felt some peace, and I spent many hours there repeating that strange prayer, "My God, if you exist, let me know it." The idea came to me that I should obtain some information about that religion, hoping that I might just find the truth of which I despaired. I thought the best thing would be to take a class about Catholicism, just as I had taken Arabic lessons. As I had looked for a good tutor to teach me Arabic, I went looking for an educated priest to give me some information about the Catholic religion....

Someone told me about a very distinguished priest who had studied at secular schools when he was young. I found myself in his confessional, telling him that I wasn't there for confession, as I had no faith, but that I wanted some information about the

Catholic religion.... The Good Lord, who had so forcefully begun the work of conversion in me by irresistibly drawing me to
the Church by that powerful inner grace, now brought it to com-
pletion. This priest to whom the Lord had sent me (and whom
I didn't know) became my confessor and has remained so for these
fifteen years as well as being my best friend. To his excellent
teaching ability, he added even greater virtue and goodness....

As soon as I believed there was a God, I understood that I
could do nothing else than to live for him alone. My religious vocation dates from the moment I believed. God is so great! There
is such a difference between God and all that is not God!...

In the beginning faith had to overcome many obstacles. I
who had had so many doubts didn't believe everything in one day.
At times the miracles in the Gospels seemed unbelievable. At other times I wanted to include passages from the Koran in my
prayer. But the grace of God and the counsel of my confessor dissipated these clouds.... I wanted to be a religious and to live for
God alone, to do whatever was most perfect to do, no matter
what. My confessor made me wait for three years. As for me, as
much as I wanted to pour myself out before God in total self-for-
getfulness, as Bossuet writes, I didn't know which Order to
choose. The Gospel showed me that the first commandment is
to love God with one's whole heart and that everything should be
wrapped in love. Everyone knows that the first effect of love is
imitation. Therefore, I had only to enter the Order where I found
the most exact imitation of Jesus. I didn't feel made to imitate
his public life of preaching. Therefore, I felt I should imitate the
hidden life of the humble, poor worker of Nazareth. It seemed to
me that nothing presented this as well as the Trappists.

I tenderly loved what little family God had left me. But,
wishing to make a sacrifice in imitation of him who had made
so many, I left for a Trappist monastery in Armenia about twelve
years ago. I spent six and a half years there. But in a desire to re-

semble Jesus more through greater abjection and further strip-
ping of myself, I went to Rome and received permission from the
Abbot General to leave the Order. This was to be able to go to
Nazareth and there to live alone and unknown, living from my
daily labor as a common workman. I stayed there for four years,
removed from everything, in blessed solitude and recollection. I
enjoyed that poverty and lowliness that God had made me so ardently desire in order to imitate him.

About a year ago I returned to France on the advice of my
confessor in order to receive Holy Orders. I have just been ordained and I am doing the necessary paperwork in order to continue living the hidden life of Jesus at Nazareth in the Sahara. I
don't go there to preach but to live in solitude and poverty the
humble work of Jesus. At the same time I will try to do some good
for souls not by word but through prayer, the offering of the Holy
Sacrifice, through penance and charity. By the time you receive
this I may have already left France. A White Father has just been
named Bishop of the Sahara and if he doesn't veto my plans he
might ask me to meet him in Algiers.... If not, I will be so grateful to see you again....

Why am I writing you such a long confession, my dear
friend? Because, according to the two letters that you so gra-
ciously wrote to me, it seems that there are some very slight sim-
ilarities between your state of mind and my own some fifteen
years ago. Very slight, fortunately. Your faith has only been slight-
ly shaken while mine was dead. And you have been living a virtuous life and doing good works while mine was, alas, totally the
opposite.... You will find that same infinite peace, radiant light,
and unquenchable goodness that I enjoy these last twelve years
by following the path that the good Lord had me follow. Prayer.
Pray very much. Carefully choose a good confessor and carefully follow his advice, as you would that of a good teacher. Read,
re-read and meditate on the Gospel. Try to practice it. With these

three things you can't miss quickly coming to that light that transforms everything in life and that turns earth into a heaven by unit-
ing our will to God's will. Jesus said so. It is his first word to his
apostles, his first word to all those who thirst to know him. *"Venite
et videte."* "Come and see" (Jn 1:39). "Start by coming." Then you
will "see." You will enjoy the light to the same degree that you
will have put these words into practice. *"Venite et videte."* In my
own experience, I have seen the truth of these words. I am writing you this letter to tell you so.

What does it matter if the lack of faith seems so general-
ized and that only women and children believe and pray? If our
religion is the truth, if the Gospel is the word of God, we must
believe and practice even if we were absolutely alone in doing
so. Elijah thought he was alone, but God had preserved other
souls unknown to him, who had not bent their knees to Baal....
I admire your learning. You have done more academic work than
many Benedictines. You have also discovered for yourself that you
won't find the light there. We find that through prayer: "Ask and
you will receive" (Mt 7:7). We find it by persevering with a good
confessor: "He who hears you hears me" (Lk 10:16). We find it
in the imitation of Jesus: "If someone wants to serve me, let them
follow me" (Jn 12:26). In doing these three things, we infallibly
enter into the full light of day in which we can say with David,
"nox illuminatiomea in deliciis meis" (Ps 139:12, Vulgate), because
Jesus promised that "whoever comes to me I will not reject" (Jn
6:37).

I pray for you very much. I wish I were holy enough to obtain great graces for you by my prayer. But since, alas, I have
neither virtue, knowledge, prudence, nor intelligence, and I feel
so powerless to obtain such great things for you from God, I give
you the only thing I can by trying to show you my trust and my
equally unlimited devotion.

BIBLIOGRAPHY

Rather than cite French texts that will be of little use to most readers, I have chosen to include existing references in English. While the meditations of Charles de Foucauld, most of which are from the time he spent in Nazareth, can be interesting and inspiring, they are less concrete and expressive of his actual experience than his letters. Quotes from some of these letters may be found in a number of these books.

Books about Charles de Foucauld

Antier, Jean-Jacques. *Charles de Foucauld.* San Francisco: Ignatius Press, 1999.

Bazin, René. *Charles de Foucauld "Hermit and Explorer."* London: Burns, Oates and Washbourne, 1923.

Hillyer, Philip. *Charles de Foucauld: Way of the Christian Mystics.* Vol. 9. Collegeville, MN: Liturgical Press, 1990.

Lepetit, Charles. *Two Dancers in the Desert.* Maryknoll, NY: Orbis Books, 1983.

Merad, Ali. *Christian Hermit in an Islamic World.* Mahwah, NJ: Paulist Press, 1999.

Six, Jean François. *Spiritual Autobiography of Charles de Foucauld.* Denville, NJ: Dimension Books, 1964.

Writings of Charles de Foucauld

de Foucauld, Charles. *Charles de Foucauld: Scriptural Meditations on Faith*. Brooklyn, NY: New City Press, 1988.

————. *Charles de Foucauld: Hope in the Gospels*. Brooklyn, NY: New City Press, 1990.

————. *Meditations of a Hermit*. Maryknoll, NY: Orbis Books, 1981.

————. *Charles de Foucauld: Inner Search: Letters 1889–1916*. Maryknoll, NY: Orbis Books, 1979.

Ellsberg, Robert (ed.). *Charles de Foucauld: Writings Selected with an Introduction by Robert Ellsberg*. Maryknoll, NY: Orbis Books, 1999.

Video

Seeds of the Desert: The Legacy of Charles de Foucauld. 38 min. By the Little Brothers of the Gospel and the Little Sisters of Jesus, USA, 1998.

PERMISSIONS
ACKNOWLEDGMENTS

Charles de Foucauld, *Lettres à Mme de Bondy* © Desclée de Brouwer, 1966. Used with permission.

L'aventure de l'amour de Dieu. Jean-François Six © Éditions du Seuil, 1993; *Lettres et Carnets.* Jean François Six © Éditions du Seuil, 1995; *Itinéraire Spirituel de Charles de Foucauld. Oeuvres Spirituelle.* © Éditions du Seuil, 1958. Used with permission.

La Bonté de Dieu © Nouvelle Cité, 1996; *La Dernière Place* © Nouvelle Cité, 1974; *Carnet de Tamanrasset, August 11, 1905* © Nouvelle Cité, 1986; *Charles de Foucauld—explorateur au Maroc, ermite au Sahara,* René Bazin © Nouvelle Cité, 2003; *Imitation du Bien Aimé* © Nouvelle Cité, 1997; *Lettres à un Ami de Lycée* © Nouvelle Cité, 1982; *Meditations sur les psaumes* © Nouvelle Cité, 1980; *Qui peut résisterà Dieu* © Nouvelle Cité, 1980; *Reglements et Directoire* © Nouvelle Cité, 1995; *Voyager dans la Nuit* © Nouvelle Cité, 1979; *En vue de Dieu Seul* © Nouvelle Cité, 1973. Used with permission.

Correspondances Sahariennes © Éditions du Cerf, 1998; *Lettres à mes frères de la Trappe* © Éditions du Cerf, 1991. Used with permission.

Photos courtesy of the Little Sisters of the Poor, Rome (Tre Fontane), used with permission of the Office of the Postulator of the Cause for the Canonization of Charles de Foucauld and of the de Blic Family (family of Charles de Foucauld's sister).

BOOKS & MEDIA

The Daughters of St. Paul operate book and media centers at the following addresses. Visit, call or write the one nearest you today, or find us on the World Wide Web, www.pauline.org

CALIFORNIA

3908 Sepulveda Blvd, Culver City, CA 90230	310-397-8676
5945 Balboa Avenue, San Diego, CA 92111	858-565-9181
46 Geary Street, San Francisco, CA 94108	415-781-5180

FLORIDA

145 S.W. 107th Avenue, Miami, FL 33174	305-559-6715

HAWAII

1143 Bishop Street, Honolulu, HI 96813	808-521-2731
Neighbor Islands call:	866-521-2731

ILLINOIS

172 North Michigan Avenue, Chicago, IL 60601	312-346-4228

LOUISIANA

4403 Veterans Memorial Blvd, Metairie, LA 70006	504-887-7631

MASSACHUSETTS

885 Providence Hwy, Dedham, MA 02026	781-326-5385

MISSOURI

9804 Watson Road, St. Louis, MO 63126	314-965-3512

NEW JERSEY

561 U.S. Route 1, Wick Plaza, Edison, NJ 08817	732-572-1200

NEW YORK

150 East 52nd Street, New York, NY 10022	212-754-1110

PENNSYLVANIA

9171-A Roosevelt Blvd, Philadelphia, PA 19114	215-676-9494

SOUTH CAROLINA

243 King Street, Charleston, SC 29401	843-577-0175

TENNESSEE

4811 Poplar Avenue, Memphis, TN 38117	901-761-2987

TEXAS

114 Main Plaza, San Antonio, TX 78205	210-224-8101

VIRGINIA

1025 King Street, Alexandria, VA 22314	703-549-3806

CANADA

3022 Dufferin Street, Toronto, ON M6B 3T5	416-781-9131

¡También somos su fuente para libros, videos y música en español!